THOMAS AQUINAS

DICTIONARY

THOMAS AQUINAS DICTIONARY

Edited by

MORRIS STOCKHAMMER

With an Introduction by Theodore E. James

PHILOSOPHICAL LIBRARY

New York

This dictionary is based on Aquinas' *Opera Omnia* (1882) and on two English translations by Joseph Rickaby, S. J., namely, *Aquinas Ethicus* (Burns and Oates, New York, 1896); *Of God and His Creatures* (Burns & Oates, London, 1905). References with the initials C. G. belong to *The Summa Contra Gentiles;* references without any letters are taken from *The Summa Theologiae.*

INTRODUCTION

St. Thomas Aquinas was born about 1225 in the castle of Roccasecca, in the county of Aquino, about 78 miles from Rome. He was the youngest son of Landulph, count of Aquino, and Theodora, a Neapolitan noblewoman of Norman ancestry. At an early age he was dedicated to the service of God, as an oblate of St. Benedict at the monastery of Montecassino. There he was trained in the fundamentals of the spiritual life and was educated in the monastery school in the arts of reading and writing. For about eight years calligraphy and the trivium of grammar (including excerpts of the literary works of Aesop, Ovid, Horace, Vergil, etc.), rhetoric (Cicero and Quintilian) and elementary logic (probably the *logica vetera*) were parts of the secular learning to which was given the time remaining from a study of the Psalms, readings from the Sacred Scriptures and the exercises of the monastic life. Having completed the elements of classical learning he was sent to the recently founded University of Naples, where he pursued advanced work in the trivium under Peter Martin and began serious study of the quadrivium (arithmetic, geometry, astronomy and music) and natural philosophy under the tutelage of Peter of Ireland, who was also proficient in the knowledge of Greek. Providentially, Frederick II had ordered that the natural philosophy in the University be based on Aristotle and his commentators. It is probably here that Thomas first met the works of the Philosopher, *il maestro di color che sanno,* perhaps in the then recently (1231) translated version of Michael Scot. After four years of university work he joined the Order of Preachers contrary to the wishes of his parents, who apparently had hopes of their son being Abbot of Montecassino some day. Theodora set out for Naples to change his mind, but when she arrived there Thomas was already on his way to Rome by another route. She followed and demanded that Thomas be released from the Dominicans, but again she was unable to talk to Thomas, who was by now on his way to Paris. Theodora was not to be frustrated. She contacted two older sons in the army of Frederick II, had them intercept Thomas, and return him to the family hearth. For over a year he spent time reading the *Bible*, the *Book of Sentences* of Peter Lombard and the logical works of Aristotle, when he was not trying to justify his vocation to the Dominicans and receive the consent of his family. He finally won out and was permitted to become a Friar Preacher under the banner of St. Dominic. After a short stay in Naples he was transferred to Rome and then sent by way of Paris to the *studium generale* at Cologne.

Any accurate chronology of these student years is impossible. It is quite sure that he did not begin studies in Cologne under Albert the Great before the year 1248. So between 1245, when he was released from confinement and allowed to pursue his Dominican vocation, and 1248, he probably filled out his year of novitiate and finished his philosophical preparation for Theology, although where, we don't know. From 1248-1252 he studied Theology under Albert, the *Doctor Universalis*, who was revered as a great scholar in every branch of knowledge by such men as Roger Bacon, Ulrich of Strasburg, Pope Alexander IV and Dante Alighieri. From the many accounts of this four year period it is quite clear that Thomas' time was not confined to theology in the narrow sense. Albert's interest in the scientific and philosophic understanding of nature led to many courses of a more secular type in which the writings of Aristotle and other *authorities* of the past were employed. When Thomas had completed his training at Cologne he was chosen to be a *Bachelor* at the *studium generale* in Paris, lecturing on the Bible. After about two years in this capacity he became a *baccalaureus sententiarius*, reading the *Book of the Sentences* of Peter of Lombard (d. 1180). From the years 1250-56 date the composition of his *De Ente et Essentia, Commentary on the Book of Sentences* and, perhaps, the *De Principiis Naturae*. In 1256, though he had not reached the age of 35 as prescribed by university regulations, he became a Master of Theology and continued his teaching and writing at Paris. Among his works at this time we find the *Commentary on the De Trinitate of Boethius*, which contains Thomas' ideas on the division and methods of the sciences, and the beginnings of the treatise *Summa Contra Gentiles* (On the Truth of the Christian Faith).

After three years, in 1259, Thomas returned to Italy, was made a Preacher General, attended several provincial chapters and continued his teaching at the Papal Court of Urban IV at Orvieto (1261-65). During this period is assigned the *Exposition of the*

Gospels (Catena Aurea), the conclusion of the *Contra Gentiles*, several minor works and the great literary and spiritual masterpiece *The Office of Corpus Christi*, which contains the popular hymns *Pange Lingua* and *Lauda Sion*. The latter work earned for Thomas the title of "the poet and theologian of the Eucharist." From 1265-67 he directed the house of studies at S. Sabina in Rome, and from 1267-68 he was at Viterbo with Clement IV. In both places he found the leisure which fructified into commentaries on the physical works of Aristotle, random questions in theology and the First Part of the *Summa Theologiae*. On his way back to Paris he gave Lenten sermons at Bologna and Milan and resumed teaching in January of 1269. From then until 1272 he was involved in the many problems of the academic life: lecturing, presiding at disputations, composing commentaries on other works of Aristotle in the fields of metaphysics, ethics, logic and politics, and working to finish the *Summa*. He became embroiled in the discussions about the Aristotelian position on the nature of the soul, in which he disagreed with John Peckham and publicly defended the *orthodox* Aristotelian philosophy against the Latin Averroists, mainly Siger of Brabant. His treatises *On the Unity of the Intellect* and *On the Eternity of the World* were probably instrumental in the condemnation of Averroism in 1270. Shortly thereafter he was recalled to Naples, where he lectured on the *Psalms* and the *Epistles* of St. Paul. He also found time to write commentaries on Aristotle's *De Caelo et Mundo* and *On Generation and Corruption*, Thomas' last philosophical composition. He preached on *The Apostles' Creed*, the *Our Father*, *The Ten Commandments* and *The Hail Mary*. His health was failing more and more at this time and it became so bad that he gave up all writing and dictation. In the early months of 1274 Thomas set out for the Council of Lyons at the special invitation of the Pope. Along the way he became seriously ill and was carried to the Benedictine monastery of Fossanova, where he died on March 7, 1274. He was canonized in 1323 by Pope John XXII, declared *Angelic Doctor* of the Church by Pius V in 1567 and made *Patron of Catholic Schools* by Leo XIII in 1880. In 1918 the Code of Canon Law made a study of his philosophy and theology obligatory in Catholic seminaries; in 1923 Pope Pius XI exalted him as *Ducem Studiorum;* Pius XII extols his principles, wisdom and method in the Encyclical *Humani Generis*.

There is no doubt that the philosophy and theology of Thomas

Aquinas went through a variety of stages of expansion, adjustment, contraction and development. This is quite evident when one compares an early work like the *Commentary on the Book of Sentences* with the *Summa Theologiae*, or the *De Ente* with the later Opuscula and Commentaries. Nevertheless, in spite of such development over the years, there is discernible a deeper and deeper refinement and a richer expansion of what could be called the mind of the Angelic Doctor. One aspect of it is revealed in his Scriptural commentaries: in *Isaias*, in the *Evangelists*, in *Jeremiah*, in *Job*, in the *Psalms*, in the *Epistles* of Paul; another facet sparkles in his commentaries on *The Sentences*, on the *Hebdomadibus* and *de Trinitate* of Boethius and on the *Divine Names* of Dionysius; a philosophical latitude is exposed by the commentaries on Aristotle's *On the Soul, On Sense and the Sensed, On Memory and Reminiscence, On the Metaphysics, On the Physics, On the Ethics, On Meteorology, On Interpretation, On the Posterior Analytics, On the Politics, On the Heaven and the Earth, On Generation and Corruption* and the commentary on *The Book of Causes* by Proclus; a personal depth is seen in the Opuscula, like *On Being and Essence* or *On the Principles of Nature, On the Rule of Princes, The Compendium of Theology, On the Unity of the Intellect Against the Averroists* and *On the Eternity of the World,* to mention but a few; the disputed questions *On Truth, On the Power of God, On Spiritual Creatures, On the Soul, On Evil, On the Virtues* show his own clarity of excellence to an even greater degree; the greatest achievement is seen in the two great *Summae*, in which philosophy and theology are dynamically related through distinct disciplines from both the formally objective and methodological point of view.

The *Summa Contra Gentiles* (On the Truth of the Christian Faith) is, as the title indicates, a formal treatise in theology in which we find philosophy performing its function as a devoted hand-maiden. According to the legend, Thomas composed it at the request of Raymond of Penafort as a missionary primer to be used among the Moors in Spain. It was begun in Paris before 1259 and completed in Orvieto before 1264. The first three books give a philosophical account and defense of certain positions or beliefs found in the Christian Faith. The reasonableness of the foundations and ingredients of the faith are shown. The fourth book elaborates theologically those teachings of the Faith which cannot be discovered or proved by philosophy, e.g. The Trinity, Incarnation, Sacraments etc. In detail the first two books deal with the existence and nature of God, the third with the return of all creatures to their end and source, God, the fourth book deals with the mysteries of faith clarified by scriptural references and positive theology. The method of presentation is by way of declarative exposition or by the elucidation of a thesis simply stated as a part of Christian Faith, a method quite appropriate to a primer. Since this varies from the method of the opuscula, from the method of the *Summa Theologiae,* and from the method of the philosophical and theological commentaries, it is quite evident that St. Thomas did not think that any one method was absolutely supreme, but rather was convinced of the Aristotelian principles that the method should be proportional to the subject-matter and the type of investigation involved.

The *Summa Theologiae,* begun in 1266 and unfinished at his death, is, perhaps, the most mature of Thomas' works from the philosophical and theological viewpoint. And, it is interesting to note, it was written expressly for *beginners* in theology or sacred science. Its method, format, economy, order of contents, language and spirit are perfectly adapted to the subject-matter and his purpose. One is well aware of being in the presence of a master architect when he reads through the orderly development of the over-all plan and of the minor details essential to the realization of that plan. Thomas aims "to treat of the things which belong to the Christian religion in such a way as befits the instruction of beginners. . . . With confidence in God's help, we shall try, following the needs of the subject-matter, to set forth briefly and clearly the things which pertain to sacred doctrine."

Obviously this is another work in theology. Philosophy is utilized insofar as it can help in the understanding of those things which belong to the Christian religion. It is divided by Thomas into three parts, though someone later divided the second part into two, because of its length, for convenience of binding or some other practical purpose. Part One treats of God in Himself and as the source of things. Part Two is the way of return of man to his source, which is his goal. Part Three gives the means by which man may reach his goal and the precise nature of that goal. The division of the contents clarifies the over-all plan and purpose. In contrast with the pedagogical method he used as a *Bachelor,* that of reading the text of the

Bible or of the Sentences and elaborating a series of glosses or explications, and in contrast with the isolated format of the disputed question, Thomas adapts a variation of the disputed question as a dialectical preparation for the solution of a problem seen in the over-all context of its relation to God as efficient and final cause of all. Each article presents a precise problem for investigation in the form of a dialectical question, e.g. whether God exists? After several arguments are given for one possible answer, and usually one answer to the opposite position, there is a dialectical determination of the range and depth of the problem as a propaedeutic to a demonstrative resolution where such is possible. In cases, because of the type of problem, the preferred solution to the question remains in the area of probability. After the resolution of the dialectical question is completed the article closes with a reflective review of the original arguments contra (usually called objections), with reasons expressly given for their rejection or why they are less probable. Thus each article is a neat unit in the over-all plan for understanding as much as possible the ingredients of the Christian Faith. Thomas' science of theology integrates the formal principles of the Aristotelian logic of science with the Neo-platonic theory of emanation and return, and the contingent requirements of the Judeo-Christian history of salvation. The *Summa Theologiae* is a Christian edifice of the divine plan of God as source and goal of man, with the God-Man as model, way and life for the return. God is the Alpha *and* Omega.

Though the *Summa* is a work prepared especially for beginners in the formal science of theology it presupposes that the students are factually familiar with the basic teachings of the Christian Faith. It, also, presupposes a familiarity with the philosophical background of discussions of topics related to sacred science. Only on such presuppositions would the dialectical method of investigation be as fruitful as it is. When we reflect on the total philosophical presentation found in the *Summae* and correlate it with his ideas found in other theological and philosophical works, we are amazed at the scientifically arranged "systems" which appear. He overwhelms us with the precision of his conceptions and the artistry of their integration. His philosophy is a thing of beauty which delights the mind when we contemplate it.

Central to this work of art is his understanding of being as that whose perfection of fulfillment is to exist. Epistemologically it is the sensio-intellectual judgment which functions as a means for the grasp of being as presented in human experience. The varieties of beings indicate the multiplicity of types of being and lead to an acknowledgment of the analogous nature of being when they are applied to substances and the nine varieties of accidents. In experience every object is finite, limited either as regards participation in being in the order of kinds or as individuals in a precise kind. Objects of experience are involved in change of incidental characteristics (accidents) and subject to generation and corruption. They are examples of grades of perfection and are united into an order called the universe. The characteristics of change, grades of being and ordered arrangement indicate a radical dependence in the order of existing upon a Being which is Existence Itself, God. With the factual recognition of such a reality, one can see clearly the starting point of the evolution of all things; an acceptance of the existential, essential and causal attributes of God known by way of negation and analogy brings into focus the fact of a free production of creatures by way of creation, providence over them and government of their activities by which the individual and collective goals are achieved. The universe of creatures is, also, a work of art by the supreme Artist.

Foremost among the inhabitants of this planet is man touching the world of pure spirit with his soul and sharing in the limitations of matter in motion because of his body. An understanding of the nature of man is a pre-requisite for a determination of what his existential purpose is and how he must act in order to reach his Omega. An intelligently free being is open to the whole range of created being and his capacities can only be completely filled by the Supreme Being itself. A human goal can be reached by means of human acts; man's supernatural goal of active contemplative love of God in a face-to-face vision is realized by a divine transformation in grace, a created participation in the divine nature itself. Alpha and Omega, nature and grace, alienation and return, predestination and choice, misery and happiness, sinner and saint, animal and spirit, life in death and death in life, are resolvable paradoxes when integrated into Thomas' view of philosophy and theology.

Manhattan College   Theodore E. James

xi

EDITOR'S PREFACE

Ranking among the most comprehensive systematicians of theological thought, Thomas Aquinas, the bulwark of Scholasticism, looked into virtually every corner of the theological edifice. "There are two sorts of . . ." This and phrases similar to it are constant expressions repeated on almost every page of Thomas' masterwork, *Summa Theologiae.* They are vivid reflections of his investigative method, a method which consisted of a broad and liberal vision that scrutinized all facets of each issue considered by him throughout his writings.

It would be presumptuous at best to expect to extract all the decisive quotations from the vast body of Aquinas' literature. And yet, without the hope of possibly accomplishing this task, one could not endeavor to compile a dictionary on Thomas Aquinas.

In the preparation of this volume, therefore, I was constantly reminded of Rickaby's admonition:

> St. Thomas is an author peculiarly liable to misrepresentation by taking his words in one place to the neglect of what he says on the same subject elsewhere. No one is safe in quoting him who has not read much of him. (Ethics, I, p. 131).

Naturally, the dictionary is organized with this in mind. I have sought to make misrepresentation a moot point and to distill and deliver the Thomist philo-theology within a framework of its essentials. In addition, only entries that are of interest to the modern reader were included, whereas items of merely medieval concern were omitted.

M.S.

A

ABSTINENCE

Abstinence helps to the gathering of wisdom.
II-II, q. 148, a. 6.

The good of reason cannot be in man, if he abstain from all pleasures.
II-II q. 142, a. 1, §2.

Some abstain for the health of their bodies.
II-II, q. 142, a. 1.

Abstinence by its name implies a subtraction of food.
II-II, q. 146, a. 1.

ABSTRACTION

There are two kinds of abstraction: the abstraction of the general from the particular, and the abstraction of the form from the matter.
I, q. 40, a. 3.

ACCIDENT

That which is outside the substance of a thing, and yet is belonging to the thing, is called an accident of it.
I-II, q. 7, a. 1.

That whose nature it is to exist in another.
I, q. 28, a. 2c.

ACCUSATION

A man ought not to proceed to accusation except upon a point that he is altogether sure of, so that ignorance of fact can have no place there.
II-II, q. 68, a. 3, §1.

Sometimes one is moved to accuse by a justifiable error.
II-II, q. 68, a. 3, §1.

Sometimes one proceeds to accusation from mere levity of mind, too easily believing what one hears, and that is rashness.
II-II, q. 68, a. 3, §1.

In the dignity of his person, a neighbor is injured openly by a judicial accusation, or by abusive language addressed to him.
II-II, q. 61, a. 3.

ACT

The act to which operative power is compared is operation.
I, q. 54, a. 3c.

Act, however, is duplex: first and second; first act is the form and integrity of a thing; second act is operation.
I, q. 48, a. 5c.

What is in potency is reduced to act only by a being in act.
I, q. 3, a. 1c.

There is nothing to hinder one act having two effects, of which one only is in the intention of the agent, while the other is beside his intention.
II-II, q. 64, a. 7.

There is a twofold act of the will, one immediately belonging to and elicited by the will itself; another commanded by the will and exercised through the medium of some other power, as walking and speaking, which are commanded by the will and exercised by means of the motive power.
I-II, q. 6, a. 4.

The interior act of the will and the exterior act, are morally one act.
I-II, q. 20, a. 3.

An act is human by being voluntary. Now a human act is evil for want of due proportion to some measure.
I-II, q. 71, a. 6.

Every act must be proportioned both to the object and to the agent. From the object it has its species: from the strength of the agent it has the measure of its intensity.
II-II, q. 26, a. 7.

In human acts the ends in view are as the principles in speculation.
1-11, q. 57, a. 4.

That act is properly human which is under the control of man.
I, q. 1, a. 4, a. 6c.

Acts done with delight are done with more attention and perseverance. But an extraneous delight would impede activity by distracting the attention.
I-II, q. 4, a. 1, §3.

ACT, GREAT
It is indeed a great act, relatively speaking, to make an excellent use of a trifle. But speaking absolutely, that is a great act which uses a grand thing excellently.
II-II, q. 129, a. 1.

ACT, MORAL
Moral acts stand in a different category from the performances of art. In the performances of art reason is directed to a particular end, which is something devised by reason: in moral performances it is directed to the general end of all human life.
I-II, q. 21, a. 2, §2.

ACT, PURE
God is pure act, receiving nothing from another, having no diversity in himself.
I, q. 90, a. 1c.

ACTION
The continued action of anything increases its effect.
I-II, q. 32, a. 2.

We are guided by knowledge to actions.
II-II, q. 166, a. 1.

Of the actions done by man, those alone are properly called human, which are proper to man as man. Now man differs from irrational creatures in this, that he is master of his own acts. Wherefore those acts alone are properly called human, whereof man is master.
I-II, q. 1, a. 1.

Action is twofold. There is one variety that proceeds from the agent to exterior matter, as the action of cutting and burning, and such an activity is a transient act of the patient. There is another action immanent, or remaining in the agent himself, as feeling, understanding, and willing.
I-II, q. 3, a. 2, §3.

ACTIVE
In the operations of the active life the lower powers concur, which are common to us with the dumb animals. However, in

some particular cases, the active life is rather to be chosen for the necessity of our present life.
II-II, q. 182, a. 1.

ACTIVITY

It is manifest that activity is the last and crowning act of an active being. And hence it is that each thing is said to be for the sake of its activity. It needs must be therefore that the happiness of man is a certain activity.
I-II, q. 3. a. 2.

Activities are pleasant inasmuch as they are proportionate and connatural to the agent. But any activity exceeding that measure ceases to be proportionate or pleasant, and becomes rather laborious and wearisome.
I-II, q 32, a. 1, §3.

We gain fitting good by some activity; also the very activity itself that is proper to the agent is a certain fitting good. Hence all pleasure must follow upon some activity.
I-II, q. 32, a. 1.

Pleasure perfects activity as an active cause.
I-II, q. 34, a. 4.

ACTUALLY

He who has sown seed in his land has not yet got the harvest actually, but only virtually.
I-II, q. 62, a. 4, §1.

ADJUSTED

Things that are equalized are said to be adjusted.
II-II, q. 57, a. 1.

ADMONITION

Secret admonition should precede public denunciation.
II-II, q. 33, a. 7.

ADORATION

Even corporal adoration is in spirit, inasmuch as it proceeds from spiritual devotion and is directed to it.
II-II, q. 84, a. 2, §1.

A definite place is chosen for adoration, not for the sake of the God who is adored, as though He had local bounds, but for the sake of the adorers themselves.
II-II, q. 84, a. 3, §2.

4

ADULTERY
A man is injured by his wife in adultery, and that secretly for the most part.
II-II, q. 61, a. 3.

In adultery there is a twofold sin against chastity and the good of human generation: first, inasmuch as the adulterer cohabits with a woman not joined with him in wedlock, thus neglecting what is requisite for the good education of his own offspring; again, because he cohabits with a woman that is joined in wedlock with another man, thus hindering the good of another man's offspring.
II-II, q. 154, a. 8.

ADVICE
One takes advice in order to find out what is good for him.
I, q. 19, a. 7.

AFFABILITY
A man must be suitably ordered and adapted to his fellow-men in social intercourse as well in action as in word, that he may behave to each appropriately. And therefore there must be a special virtue that observes this suitable order; and it is called friendliness, or affability.
II-II, q. 114, a. 1.

AFFAIRS, HUMAN
Human affairs are handled in more orderly fashion, where every individual has his own care of something to look to; whereas there would be confusion if every one indiscriminately took the management of anything he pleased.
II-II, q. 66, a. 2.

AFFIRMATION
In an affirmation there is understood the denial of the opposite statement.
II-II, q. 107, a. 2.

AFFLICTION
One is sometimes afflicted without fault, but not without cause.
II-II, q. 108, a. 4.

A man is sometimes afflicted in temporal goods without his fault; this is the case in many of the tribulations of the present life, divinely inflicted to prove a man or to humble him.
II-II, q. 108, a. 4.

5

AGENT

An agent does not act without a purpose.
I, q. 7, a. 4.

AGENT, INTELLECTUAL

Only intellectual agents can act with free judgment.
I, q. 59, a. 3.

AIR

Air is colorless, and becomes luminous only through light.
I, q. 67, a. 3.

Air is transparent.
I, q. 48, a. 4.

ALMS

The religious men on whose churches endowments are bestowed by the munificence of princes or other faithful, may live thereupon without laboring with their hands; and yet it is certain that they live by alms.
II-II, q. 187, a. 4.

Whatever movable goods are bestowed on religious men by the faithful, they may lawfully live thereupon: for it is folly to say that one may receive great possessions in alms, and not a piece of bread or a little money. The use of gifts would be rendered unlawful to them if they were to desist from the acts of religion, because in that case they would defraud the purpose of the donors.
II-II, q. 187, a. 4.

ALMSGIVING

It is not lawful to steal in order to give alms.
II-II, q. 110, a. 3, §4.

There is a time at which one sins mortally in omitting to give alms: on the part of the receiver, when there is an apparent, evident, and urgent need, and no appearance of any one at hand to relieve it: on the part of the giver, when he has superfluities, which are not necessary to him in his present state, according to a probable estimate.
II-II, q. 32, a. 5, §3.

It is of precept to give alms out of your superfluity, and to give alms to him who is in extreme need: otherwise almsgiving is matter of counsel, as there are counsels of every better good.
II-II, q. 32, a. 5.

To will and to work a person's good, it is requisite that we should

6

succour his need, which is done by almsgiving; and therefore almsgiving is of precept. Almsgiving is an act necessary to virtue, or in other words, required by right reason.
II-II, q. 32, a. 5.

ALTRUISM
A man is bound in charity to love himself more than his neighbor. A sign of this is, that a man ought not to take upon himself any evil of sin to deliver his neighbor from sin.
II-II, q. 26, a. 4.

AMBITION
Ambition means an inordinate craving after honor: hence plainly ambition is always a sin.
II-II, q. 131, a. 1.

Ambition is opposed by excess to magnanimity.
II-II, q. 131, a. 2, §1.

AMBIVALENCE
One can desire and not desire the same thing.
I, q. 64, a. 3, §1.

AMOR DEI
We approach God, not by corporeal, but by spiritual affection.
I, q. 3, a. 1, §5.

AMORAL
A man is sometimes neither good nor bad.
I, q. 20, a. 4, §5.

A thing that had no being nor goodness in it, could be called neither evil nor good.
I-II, q. 18, a. 1.

AMPUTATION
If it be expedient for the welfare of the whole human body that some member should be amputated, as being rotten and corrupting the other members, the amputation is wholesome.
II-II, q. 64, a. 2.

A physician of the body gives help to his patient, if he can, without amputation of any limb; but if he cannot, he amputates the limb that is less necessary, that the life of the whole may be preserved.
II-II, q. 33, a. 7.

AMUSEMENT
The first and principal thing is, that amusement be not sought for

in actions or words that are unseemly or hurtful.
II-II, q. 168, a. 2.

ANALOGOUS
Some words are used of God and creatures in an analogous sense, that is, according to proportion.
I. q. 13, a. 5.

ANGEL
The highest angel fell into sin with greater intensity than the lower angels.
I, q. 63, a. 8, §3.

ANGELIC
The angelic intellect comprehends the peculiar value ideas.
1, q. 85, a. 1. (Ed. note: Since terminology is not the business of philosophy, the intellect can be called spiritual, divine, human, or angelic.)

ANGER
Looking at things exactly as they are, no man is ever angry with himself.
I-II, q. 46, a. 7, §2.

As a great fire is soon out, having consumed all the fuel, so anger soon dies away.
I-II, q. 48, a. 2, §2.

The passion of anger is especially excited when a sufferer thinks himself ill-treated unjustly.
II-II, q. 65, a. 2, §1.

Anger is a desire of vengeance.
I-II, q. 46, a. 4.

There is required for anger some act of reason, along with an impediment to reason. Hence the Philosopher says: "They who are very drunk do not get angry, as having nothing left of the use of reason; but only when slightly intoxicated, men get angry, as having the use of reason, though impeded."
I-II, q. 46, a. 4. §3.

It is the part of anger to assault the vexatious object; and thus anger lends direct cooperation to fortitude in making the attack.
II-II, q. 123, a. 10, §3.

It is the peculiarity of the passion of anger not to have any contrary, either in the way of approach and retirement, or according to the contrariety of good and evil. The motion of anger can have no motion contrary to it; its only opposite is cessation from motion.
I-II, q. 23, a. 3.

The object of anger and of hatred is the same in substance, for as the hater wishes evil to him whom he hates, so does the angry man to him with whom he is angry, but the way of looking at it is not the same, for the hater wishes evil to his enemy as evil, but the angry man wishes evil to him with whom he is angry, not inasmuch as it is evil, but inasmuch as it bears a character of goodness, that is, inasmuch as he reckons it to be a piece of just vengeance.
I-II, q. 46, a. 6.

Evil may be found in anger, when one is angry overmuch or too little, beside the mark of right reason. But if one is angry according to right reason, then to get angry is praiseworthy.
II-II, q. 158, a. 1.

Anger seems to be the least of sins: for anger desires some penal evil in the light of something good, as a just vengeance. Hence it appears that hatred is more grievous than envy, and envy than anger. But in respect of inordinateness of manner, anger goes beyond other sins for the violence and rapidity of its movement.
II-II, q. 158, a. 4.

The anger that we speak of in God is not a passion, but a judgment of justice, inasmuch as it is His will to take vengeance on sin.
I-II, q. 47, a. 1, §1.

ANIMAL
Man is a social animal.
II-II, q. 109, a. 3, §1.

Man can know future rain from some animal movements.
I, q. 86, a. 4, §3.

Dumb animals are destitute of reason, inasmuch as by natural instinct through the imagination they are moved to something resembling the works of reason.
I-II, q. 46, a. 7, §1.

In the state of innocence man did not use animals for practical purposes but for experimental knowledge of them.
I, q. 96, a. 1, §3.

The distinction between the rational and the irrational divides the animals.
I, q. 77, a. 3.

Certain animals show enmity to one another, as the wolf and the sheep.
I, q. 96, a. 1.

Certain animals at birth can use their members.
I, q. 99, a. 1.

Land animals are more developed than fishes and birds.
I, q. 71, a. 1.

Dumb animals act from unfree judgment.
I. q. 59, a. 3.

Men should use animals, which cannot be without putting them to death.
II-II, q. 64, a. 1.

All animals exist for the sake of man.
II-II, q. 64, a. 1.

The term voluntariness may be extended to agents in which there is some approach to will: and in this way voluntariness is attributed to the actions of dumb animals, inasmuch as they are guided to their end by a sort of knowledge.
I-II, q. 6, a. 2, §2.

ANIMATE
Living things are called animate, non-living things inanimate.
I, q. 75, a. 1.

ANT
The ant has a solicitude suitable to the season; and this is what is proposed to us for imitation.
II-II, q. 55, a. 7, §1.

APPANAGE
What is part and parcel of a thing, always takes precedence over what is a mere appanage of the same.
II-II, q. 162, a. 6.

APPEAL
There are two motives that may move a man to appeal. One is confidence in the justice of his cause; and on that motive it is lawful to appeal. Another is desire to throw delays in the way of a just sentence being pronounced against him; and that is a fraudulent defence, which is unlawful: for it wrongs both the judge, whose office it impedes, and the adversary, whose just claim it does its best to upset.
II-II, q. 69, a. 3.

APPETITE
Appetite has no regard for reason.
II-II, q. 142, a. 2.

The pleasure of the sensitive appetite is attended by a certain

bodily alteration, while the pleasure of the intellectual appetite is nothing else than a simple movement of the will.
I-II, q. 31, a. 4.

The appetite is more vehemently affected towards a present than towards an absent thing.
I-II, q. 33, a. 3.

Reason controls not only the passions of the sensitive appetite, but also the operations of the intellectual appetite, or will, which is not the subject of passion.
I-II, q. 59, a. 4.

Because we are called just in this that we do a thing rightly, and the proximate principle of action is the appetitive faculty, some portion of the appetitive faculty must be the subject of justice. Now the appetitive faculty is twofold: the will, which is in the reason; and the sensitive appetite that follows the apprehension of sense, which sensitive appetite is divided into irascible and concupiscible.
II-II, q. 58, a. 4.

APPRECIATION
Whoever does not appreciate a thing great, is neither very glad if he gets it, nor very much grieved if he loses it.
II-II, q. 129, a. 8, §3.

APPREHENSION
The apprehension of reason and imagination is more profound than the apprehension of sense.
I-II, q. 35, a. 7.

APPREHENSION, SENSUAL
The apprehension of sense does not attain to the general notion of good, but to some particular good. But the intellect grasps the universal idea of good.
I-II, q. 4, a. 2, §2.

APPROPRIATION
The retainer of another man's goods ought not to appropriate them to himself, but either preserve them for restitution at a fit time, or hand them over to another for safer custody.
II-II, q. 62, a. 5, §1.

ARDUOUSNESS
The difficulty that comes of the arduousness of the work, adds to the perfection of the virtue.
II-II, q. 184, a. 8, §6.

ARISTOTLE

Aristotle, like Plato, considered as the highest human happiness the possession of spiritual science, that is, of the knowledge of value ideas.
I, q. 88, a. 1.

Aristotle was of the opinion that the body does not share in the valid reasoning of the intellect.
I, q. 84, a. 6.

Aristotle agreed with Plato that intellect and sense differ from one another. But he maintained that the sense is not an act of the soul alone, but also of the body.
I, q. 84, a. 6. (Ed. note: The opinion of Aristotle does, however, not differ from that of Plato.)

ARMY

In an army some guard the camp, some carry the standards, some fight with the sword.
II-II, q. 152, a. 2, §1.

ARROW

The arrow is shot at the target by the archer.
I, q. 59, a. 3.

ART

For the art it is not requisite that the artist's own activity should be good, but that he should turn out a good piece of work.
I-II, q. 57, a. 5, §1.

Art is a virtue on the same footing as speculative habits: that is to say, neither art nor speculative habits produce a good work in actual exercise, for that is proper to the virtue that perfects the appetite, but only in point of preparedness for well-doing.
I-II, q. 57, a. 3.

Art is nothing else than a right method of doing certain works, the goodness of which works consists not in any disposition of the appetitive powers of man, but in the excellence of the work itself as turned out. It is nothing to the praise of the artificer as such, with what will he goes to work, but what sort of work he produces.
I-II, q. 57, a. 3.

ARTIFICER

The artificer creates a certain object by virtue of an exemplar before him.
I, q. 44, a. 3.

ARTISTIC
Artistic goodness is looked for, not in the artist himself, but rather in the thing wrought by art.

I-II, q. 57, a. 5, §1.

AS
The term *as* does not express equality, but likeness.

I, q. 60, a. 4, §2.

ASHES
Ashes are traces of fire.

I, q. 93, a. 6.

ASSASSINATION
In the substance of his person, a neighbor is injured secretly by assassination, or by poison.

II-II, q. 61, a. 3.

ASSAULT
Assault and battery is a sort of private war between private persons, not sanctioned by any public authority, but prompted by a disordered will. And therefore an assault always involves sin.

II-II, q. 41, a. 1.

ASSENT
Assent, like consent, seems to be an act, not of understanding, but of will.

II-II, q. 2, a. 1, §8.

ASSISTANCE
Every man needs first of all the divine assistance, and secondly also human assistance, for man is naturally a social animal, not being self-sufficient for the purposes of life.

II-II, q. 129, a. 6.

ASSUAGING
Sorrow is assuaged by lamentation and groaning. Every pleasure assuages pain, and therefore the contemplation of truth assuages it, and the more so, the more perfectly one is a lover of wisdom.

I-II, q. 38, a. 2, 4.

ASTRONOMER
The astronomers foresee future eclipses with scientific accuracy.

I, q. 86, a. 4.

ATHLETE
Athletes and soldiers have to abstain from many delights to fulfil their task.

II-II, q. 142, a. 1.

ATOM

Democritus said that the material world is made by the union of atoms.
I, q. 47, a. 3.

ATTACK

One may attack by a sudden movement.
II-II, q. 123, a. 6, §1.

ATTENTION

We do that more attentively in which we take pleasure, and attention helps activity. Now when the attention is strongly fixed upon anything, it is weakened in respect of all other things, or even totally called away from them.
I-II, q. 33, a. 3.

There is a threefold attention that may be paid to vocal prayer. One is attending to the words, not to make any slip in them. The second is attending to the sense of the words. The third is attending to the end and the purpose of the prayer, that is, to God and to the object for which the prayer is offered. Sometimes this intention that carries the mind to God abounds so much that the mind forgets all other things.
II-II, q. 83, a. 13.

ATTIRE

A married woman may lawfully dress to please her husband, lest he despise her and form other connections.
II-II, q. 169, a. 2.

ATTRIBUTION

The attribution of *man* to a being implies the attribution of rationality.
I, q. 28, a. 3.

AUGUSTINE

Augustine acknowledged that spiritual values can be comprehended by the mind alone.
I, q. 88, a. 1.

Augustine often reports Plato's opinions without expressive approval.
I, q. 77, a. 5, §3.

AUTHOR, DIVINE

God is the author of nature.
I, q. 22, a. 2, §3.

AUTHOR OF VIRTUE

Man is not the author of nature, but he employs the natural things for his own, that is, virtuous purposes.

I, q. 22, a. 2, §3.

AUTHORITY

A law cannot be enacted, nor a judgment passed, except by public authority.

II-II, q. 60, a. 6.

The greater authority ought to have the greater power of coercion.

II-II, q. 65, a. 2, §2.

It belongs to the same authority to enact a law and to interpret it.

II-II, q. 60, a. 6.

AUTUMN

Autumn brings the solicitude of gathering in the fruit.

II-II q. 55, a. 7.

AVARICE

Avarice excessively strives after worldly possessions.

I, q. 63, a. 2, §2.

AVERROËS

Averroës asserts that the *agent intellect* can understand all things physical and spiritual (facts and value ideas).

I, q. 88, a. 1.

B

BASENESS

It is baser to bow to an inferior good than to a higher and better one.

II-II, q. 118, a. 5.

BEARING

The good bear with the wicked to this extent, that, so far as it is proper to do so, they patiently endure at their hands the injuries done to themselves; but they do not bear with them to the extent of enduring the injuries done to God and their neighbors.

II-II, q. 108, a. 1, §2.

BEAST

A beast is naturally distinguishable from a man.

II-II, q. 64, a. 3, §2.

Beasts do not possess reason.

I, q. 98, a. 2, §3.

BEATING

It is not lawful to beat another, except in him who has some authority over the person beaten. And because the son is subject to the authority of his father, the father may lawfully flog his son.

II-II, q. 65, a. 2.

BEATITUDE

Beatitude consists in the highest perfection of the cognitive and normative character.

I-I, q. 62, a. 1.

Beatitude of any intellectual creature denotes his understanding.

I, q. 26, a. 2.

BEAUTIFUL

That is called beautiful the mere apprehension whereof is pleasing.
I-II, q. 27, a. 1, §3.

BEAUTY

Beauty consists in proper proportion.
I, q. 5, a. 4, §1.

Beauty is eminently the attribute of chastity.
II-II, q. 152, a. 5.

Beauty in human things consists in being ordered according to reason.
II-II, q. 142, a. 2.

It belongs to the essence of beauty that the appetite should rest in the sight or knowledge of the object regarded as beautiful; hence those senses especially regard the beautiful which are the best avenues of knowledge, to wit, sight and hearing as subservient to reason.
I-II, q. 27, 1, §3.

BEFITTING

The befitting is desired for its own sake.
I, q. 5, a. 6.

BEGINNING

Not every beginning is a first beginning.
I-II, q. 6, a. 1, §1.

BEING

Being in one way signifies the entity of a thing as it is divided by the ten categories and thus it is convertible with thing. In another way being signifies the truth of a proposition, which consists in a composition and whose note is this verb 'is.' And this is the being which is used to answer the question, "is it?"
I, q. 48, a. 2, §2.

What can be, can also not be.
C.G. 1, 16, §1.

Being and understanding are different.
I, q. 34, a. 2, §1.

Even the different beings of the spiritual and the material have being in common.
I, q. 65, a. 1.

The being of a spiritual value differs from its being in the soul.
I, q. 14, a. 13, 2.

Things are not distinguished from one another in so far as they all have being, because in this they all agree. If therefore things do differ from one another, 'being' itself must be specified by certain differentias, so that different things have a different specific being (material and spiritual).
C.G. I, 26, §1.

BELIEVING
Every one easily believes that which he desires.
II-II, q. 60, a. 3.

BENEFICENCE
Beneficence becomes pleasant, inasmuch as thereby a man gets an imagination of an overflowing source of good existing in himself, whence he is able also to impart to others, which is the reason why men take pleasure in their children and in their own works, as imparting to them their own good.
I-II, q. 32, a. 6.

BENEFIT
The recipient of the benefit is bound by a debt of moral decency to some similar gratuitous payment.
II-II, q. 106, a. 6.

As in the conferring of a benefit there are two things to consider, the affection and the gift, so the same two things are to be considered in returning a benefit.
II-II, q. 106, a. 4.

BINDING
To attain to the state of liberty or slavery, there is requisite some binding or releasing: for the mere fact of one man serving another does not make him a slave, because even free men do service.
II-II, q. 184, a. 4.

BIRTH
Birth is the generation of a living creature from a joint living principle.
I, q. 27, a. 2.

BLASPHEMY
The name of blasphemy implies some disparagement of the goodness of God. If this is done in the heart only, it is blasphemy of the heart, but if it come out in speech, it is blasphemy of the mouth. And thus blasphemy is the opposite of confession of the faith.
II-II, q. 13, a. 1.

BLIND

It is some goodness in a blind man that he lives, but it is evil in him that he lacks sight. Thus a blind man has his walking power in order and is able to walk: but wanting sight to guide his steps, his walking suffers defect in that he goes stumbling.
I-II, q. 18, a. 1.

A man born blind does not have knowledge of colors.
I, q. 84, a. 3.

BOASTING

Boasting seems properly to mean a man's extolling himself and raising himself aloft in words.
II-II, q. 112, a. 1.

Boasting is opposed to truth by way of excess.
II-II, q. 112, a. 1.

Because a thing is rather to be judged according to what it is in itself than according to what it is in the opinion of others, it is more properly called boasting, when a man raises himself above what he is in himself, than when he raises himself above what he is in the opinion of others; though it may be called boasting either way.
II-II, q. 112, a. 1.

BODY

Because man cannot use reason without using the sensitive powers that require a bodily organ, man is obliged to give sustenance to his body in order to have the use of the reason.
II-II, q. 142, a. 1, §2.

The body often burdens the soul impeding the use of reason.
I, q. 101, a. 2, §1.

Seeing that man is a compound of soul and body, whatever tends to the preservation of the life of the body is some sort of good to man—though not his greatest good, because it may be put by man to an ill use.
I-II, q. 59, a 3.

Though our body cannot enjoy God to know Him and love Him, still we can arrive at the perfect enjoyment of God by the works that we do with the aid of the body. Hence there redounds upon the body from the enjoyment of the soul a certain happiness.
II-II, q. 25, a. 5, §2.

The good things of the body do not stay when they come.
I-II, q. 30, a. 4.

Two bodies cannot share the same place at the same time.
I, q. 67, a. 2.

The word *body* signifies a substance possessing three dimensions.
I, q. 18, a. 2.

BONDAGE
Real bondage is the bondage of sin.
II-II, q. 183, a. 4.

BOOK
One writes down things in material books. The knowledge of God is by analogy called the book of life or the spiritual book.
I, q. 24, a. 1.

There is no book of death, though there is a book of life.
I, q. 24, a. 1, §3.

A book without authority can be ignored with the facility with which it was written.
I, q. 77, a. 8, §1.

A book helps the memory.
I, q. 24, a. 1.

BOOK OF LIFE
There is no book of life in reference to the life of nature.
I, q. 24, a. 2, §1.

BOY
What belongs to nature in boys is to be developed and fostered: but what belongs to the deficiency of reason in them is not to be fostered, but corrected.
II-II, q. 142, a. 2, §3.

BRAVERY
Man is called brave from what is without qualification difficult.
II-II, q. 129, a. 1.

It is not from the bearing of any sort of adversity that a man is accounted absolutely a brave man, but only from bearing well the very greatest evils; from the others he gets the name of being relatively brave.
II-II, q. 123, a. 4, §1.

The brave man behaves well in dangers of any sort of death.
II-II, q. 123, a. 5.

BREATH
The breath is a means of motion.
I, q. 76, a. 7, §2.

BREATH, SPIRITUAL
To breathe (*spirare*), referring to the divine acts, means to create spiritual things.
1, q. 90, a. 1, §1. Vide Spiration.

BRUTE
Brutes always act under the influence of impressions.
I q. 57, a. 4, §3.

BUILDER
The builder can be understood as the principle of the house.
I, q. 27, a. 1, §2.

BURDENSOME
It is against reason for any one to make himself burdensome to others, making no fun himself and stopping other people's fun.
II-II, q. 168, a. 4.

BURGLAR
That man may be metaphorically styled a prudent burglar, who finds out suitable ways for committing burglary.
II-II, q. 47, a. 13.

BUYING AND SELLING
The institution of buying and selling is for the common good of both parties, each party wanting what the other has got.
II-II, q. 77, a. 1.

When a person absolutely transfers the thing that is his to another, to receive compensation in something else, it is called buying and selling.
II-II, q. 61, a. 3.

C

CALLING
For all purposes that are useful to society certain lawful callings may be appointed.
II-II, q. 168, a. 3.

CANNIBALISM
Some delight in cannibalism, or in unnatural lusts, things which are not according to human nature.
I-II, q. 31, a. 7.

CARE
One attends with greater care to what one desires more.
I, q. 91, a. 4, §1.

CAUSALITY
Causality pertains to all natural beings.
I, q. 22, a. 2. Vide Spiration.

It is clear that all the actions that proceed from any power are caused by that power acting in reference to its object.
I-II, q. 1, a. 1.

CAUSALITY, DIVINE
The causality of God is an essential attribute of a person.
I, q. 45, a. 6. (Ed. note: The divine causality is not a physical causality nor a generation, but a spiritual causality or a creation.)

CAUSE
The concept of the cause is arrived at by comparing one thing with another.
I, q. 82, a. 3, §1.

Everything corporeal that is possible to be has a cause.
C.G. I, 15, §4.

Everything is attributed rather to that which is its ordinary

cause than to that which merely affords its occasion.
II-II, q. 156, a. 1.

A material thing cannot be its own cause.
I, q. 19, a. 5. (Ed. note: But a spiritual thing can be its own reason.)

CAUSE, MATERIAL
A supreme spiritual value does not signify a material cause, but a spiritual reason.
I, q. 45, a. 1, §8.

CAUSE AND EFFECT
An effect would not be if its cause were not.
I, q. 44, a. 1, §2. Vide Spiration.

To remove the cause is to remove the effect.
I, q. 2, a. 3.

The effect does not belong to the specific essence of its cause.
II-II, q. 110, a. 1, §3.

While the cause remains, the effect remains.
I-II, q. 87, a. 3.

CAUSE AND REASON
Natural effects are not caused by spiritual reasons, but by natural causes; and causes generate only effects and not consequences.
I, q. 45, a. 2. Vide Creation and Generation.

In reference to God, the Greeks indifferently employ the words *cause* and *principle* (reason), while the Latin Teachers correctly use only the latter term.
I q. 33, a 1, §1.

CERTAINTY
Certainty is essentially opposed to suspicion.
II-II, q. 60, a. 3.

CHANCE
Certain early philosophers maintained that all things happen by chance.
I, q. 103, a. 1.

The events of chance, absolutely speaking, are not intended nor voluntary.
II-II, q. 64, a. 8.

CHANGE
Change is rendered pleasant to us, because our nature is changeable.
I-II, q. 32, a. 2.

A change acquires its value, not from the term *wherefrom* or its value-free cause, but from the term *whereto* or its valuable reason, that is, its valuable goal.
I, q. 45, a. 1, §2.

CHARITY
The greatest commandment is that of charity.
II-II, q. 44, a. 1.

Charity is a friendship.
II-II, q. 25, a. 3.

It is more praiseworthy to do a work of charity on the judgment of reason than on the mere passion of pity.
I-II, q. 24, a. 3, §1.

Charity makes a man cling to God for His own sake.
II-II, q. 17, a. 6.

CHASTITY
Chastity is concerned with the primary pleasure of the act of reproduction itself.
II-II, q. 143, a. 1.

Chastity resides in the soul as in its subject, but the matter thereof is in the body. For it belongs to chastity that, according to the judgment of reason and the choice of the will, a person should use with moderation the bodily members.
II-II, q. 151, a. 1, §1.

CHASTITY, SPIRITUAL
Where the mind of man takes delight in spiritual union with that object with which it ought to be united, namely with God, and abstains from the delight of union with other objects contrary to the due requirement of divine order, such delight and such abstinence is called spiritual chastity.
II-II, q. 151, a. 2.

CHATTEL
The son, as a son, is his father's chattel; and in like manner the slave, as a slave, is his master's chattel. But both the one and the other, considered as a man, is something subsisting by himself distinct from other beings.
II-II, q. 57, a. 4, §2.

CHILDHOOD
Notions wherewith the mind is imbued from childhood are held as firmly as if they were naturally known and self-evident.
C.G. I, 11, §1.

CHILDISH

A thing is said to be childish, either because it befits children, or else it is called childish in point of a certain likeness to a child.
II-II, q. 142, a. 2.

CHILDREN

A child pays no attention to the order of reason.
II-II, q. 142, a. 2.

A child is amended by constraint.
II-II, q. 142, a. 2.

Children imitate their parents' sins, and slaves their masters'.
II-II, q. 108, a. 4, §1.

After the child begins to have the use of reason, he begins to be his own at last, and can provide for himself in things of divine and human law; and then he is to be induced to the faith, not by compulsion, but by persuasion; and he may even consent to the faith against the will of his parents, but not before he has the use of reason.
II-II, q. 10, a. 12.

So long as a child has not the use of reason, he differs not from an irrational animal. Hence it would be against natural justice for a child to be withdrawn from his parents' care before he has the use of reason, or for any arrangement to be made about him against the will of his parents.
II-II, q. 10, a. 12.

Children differentiate between man and non-man before they differentiate between this and that man.
I, q. 85, a. 3.

In children there is most evident cause for not fasting, as well on account of the weakness of nature, for which they want frequent food and not much at a time, as also because they want much food for the necessity of growth.
II-II, q. 147, a. 4, §2.

CIRCUMSTANCE

Whatever conditions are outside the substance of an act, and yet touch somehow the human act, are called circumstances. But that which is outside of a thing, and yet is belonging to the thing, is called an accident of it. Hence the circumstances of human acts are to be called accidents of the same.
I-II, q. 7, a. 1.

CITIZEN

The virtuous citizen does not evade mortal dangers for the sake of preservation of the state.
I, q. 60, a. 5.

CLAIM

A just claim implies the proportion of one thing to another.
II-II, q. 57, a. 4.

CLEMENCY

Clemency goes to moderate the external punishment.
II-II, q. 157, a. 1.

Clemency works for the diminution of penalties, not bringing them below the standard fixed by right reason, but still below the standard of the general law which legal justice observes; clemency, however, in view of particular considerations, diminishes the penalties, and decrees that the man is not to be further punished.
II-II, q. 157, a. 2, §2.

CLERIC

Clerics ought to abstain, not only from things in themselves evil, but also from things that have the appearance of evil.
II-II, q. 77, a. 4, §3.

CLIENT

Taking up the case of poor clients is a work of mercy; and we must speak of it as of other works of mercy.
II-II, q. 71, a. 1.

CLOTHES

The use of clothes is an introduction of art.
II-II, q. 146, a. 3, 3.

CLOUD

Clouds are condensed air shaped and colored.
I, q. 51, a. 2, §3.

COERCION

No one properly is coerced by himself.
I-II, q. 96, a. 5, §3.

In human society no one has the right of coercion otherwise than by public authority.
II-II, q. 66, a. 8.

Coercion is repugnant to the coerced.
I, q. 82, a. 1.

COEXISTENCE

The power of the will does not extend to making things opposite and irreconcilable coexist.

I-II, q. 1, a. 5.

COGNITION

The object of any cognitive habit has two elements; namely, that which is materially known, which we may call the material object; and that by which the knowledge comes, which is the formal reason of the knowledge of the object.

II-II, q. 1, a. 1.

COMEDY

Comedies and tragedies feature famous men.

I, q. 29, a. 3, §2.

COMELINESS

The comeliness of man is of reason; and therefore carnal sins, whereby the flesh carries the day over reason, are fouler and more unseemly, although spiritual sins are more grievous, because they proceed from greater contempt.

II-II, q. 116, a. 2.

COMMAND

The special object of obedience is a command.

II-II, q. 104, a. 2.

COMMANDING

Whoever commands is the prime mover.

II-II, q. 62, a. 7.

COMMANDMENT

A commandment has the character of a debt.

II-II, q. 152, a. 2, §1.

The obligation of a commandment is not opposed to liberty except in him whose mind is averse to what is commanded, as appears in those who keep the commandments from fear alone.

II-II, q. 44, a. 1, §2.

COMMENCEMENT

Always the commencement of a thing is directed to the completion thereof, as is apparent both in things of nature and in things of art, and thus every commencement of perfection is directed to the attainment of perfection in its full measure.

I-II, q. 1, a. 6.

COMMENSURATE

There is a natural inclination in every agent to put forth action commensurate with its power.

II-II, q. 133, a. 1.

One thing is commensurate with another thing by convention.
II-II, q. 57, a. 2.

COMMON GOOD
The care of the common good is entrusted to rulers having public authority.
II-II, q. 64, a. 3.

COMMON SENSE
The interior or common sense is the common source of the exterior senses, harboring the power of discerning.
I, q. 78, a. 4, §1, 2.

COMMON WEAL
It is impossible for the common weal to flourish unless the citizens are virtuous, at least they who exercise sovereignty.
I-II, q. 92, a. 1, §3.

It is enough for the common weal, that the orders be virtuous to the extent of obeying the commands of those in power.
I-II, q. 92, a. 2, §3.

COMMUNITY
When a whole community has injured us, the whole community counts as one individual.
I-II, q. 46, a. 7, §3.

A community has need, not only of corporeal multiplication, but also of spiritual increase. Vide need.
II-II, q. 152, a. 2, §1.

All who are comprised in a community stand to the community as parts to the whole.
II-II, q. 58, a. 5.

Everyone living in a community is in a manner a part and member of the community; and any evil or good done him redounds to the whole body.
I-II, q. 21, a. 3.

COMPENSATION
Whoever robs or steals is bound to compensate the loss inflicted, even though he have no profit therefrom.
II-II, q. 62, a. 6.

COMPOUND
Everything that cannot be except by the concurrence of several things is compound.
C.G. I, 22, §5.

COMPREHENSION

Men comprehend spiritual things by intellect, and material things by senses.
I. q. 57, a. 2.

The intellect comprehends both the subject and the predicate together.
I. q. 58, a. 1.

Many things can be comprehended at the same time, in so far as intellectual unity permeates them.
1, q. 58, a. 1.

The senses comprehend only the external accidents of the physical things, the essences of which are comprehended only by the intellect.
I. q. 57, a. 1, §2.

What is comprehended is certainly known.
I, q. 12, a. 7.

CONCEALMENT

It would be an inordinate will for any one to wish nothing to be concealed from him by other people.
II-II, q. 40, a. 3.

It is to be observed that it is one thing to counterfeit a beauty not possessed, and another thing to conceal an ugliness arising from any cause, as from sickness or other such incident: for that concealment is lawful.
II-II, q. 169, a. 2, §2.

CONCEPT, NORMATIVE

It is a way befitting man to employ sensible signs to express his normative concepts.
II-II, q. 85, a. 1.

CONCLUSION

Conclusions are virtually contained in the first principles.
II-II, q. 44, a. 2.

CONCORD

So long as there is concord in main interests, disagreement on some little matters is not against charity.
II-II, q. 19, a. 3, §2.

CONCUPISCIBLE

The object of the concupiscible faculty is sensible good and evil, absolutely apprehended as such, that is, pleasure and pain.
I-II, q. 23, a. 1.

CONDEMNATION

An unjust condemnation is like the violence of robbers.
II-II, q. 69, a. 4.

CONDITION

Condition (implying cause and reason) is a wider term than cause.
I, q. 33, a. 1, §1.

Every condition produces its like (an effect or a consequence).
I, q. 19, a. 4.

CONDUCT

Whatever is said or done should be in keeping with the person, the season, and the place.
II-II, q. 168, a. 2.

Matters of conduct are the domain of practical reason.
I-II, q. 90, a. 2.

Conduct is an act abiding in the agent, as seeing, willing, and the like.
I-II, q. 57, a. 4.

The subject-matter of justice is exterior conduct.
II-II, q. 58, a. 11.

CONFESSION

If from open confession of the faith there ensues excitement among unbelievers, without any benefit to the faith or the faithful, it is not commendable publicly to confess the faith in such a case. But if there be hope of some benefit to the faith, or under stress of necessity, a man ought publicly to confess his faith.
II-II, q. 3, a. 2, §3.

Confessing the faith, being something affirmative, can only fall under an affirmative precept.
II-II, q. 3, a. 2.

CONFIDENCE

Where there is secure confidence of success, less solicitude comes in.
II-II, q. 55, a. 6.

CONFUTATION

To confute and rebuke may be a cause of pleasure in two ways: in one way in that it gives a man an imagination of his own wisdom and excellence; in another way in that by rebuke and reprehension one does good to another, which is pleasant.
I-II, q. 32, a 6, §3.

CONJUGAL

The conjugal act and adultery, as compared with reason, do differ in species, and have specifically different effects; because one of them deserves praise and reward, the other blame and punishment. But as compared with the generative power, they do not differ in species, and have one specific effect.
I-II, q. 18, a. 5, §3.

CONNATURAL

Sensible goods are connatural to man.
II-II, q. 168, a. 2.

CONQUEST

It is naturally pleasant to conquer, inasmuch as thereby an idea is formed of one's excellence; and therefore all games into which rivalry enters, and where victory is possible, are especially pleasant; and generally all contests according as they hold out hope of victory.
I-II, q. 32, a. 6, §3.

CONSCIENCE

A good conscience is preferable to a good name.
II-II, q. 33, a. 7.

The conscience judges what should be done or omitted.
1, q. 79, a. 13.

A bad conscience makes us have a horror of the justice for fear of punishment.
II-II, q. 44, a. 1.

In what belongs to his own person, a man ought to form his conscience by his own knowledge: but in what belongs to public authority, a man must form his conscience to what can be known in a public court of law.
II-II, q. 67, a. 2, §4.

Unjust laws are not binding in the court of conscience.
I-II, q. 96, a. 4.

Conscience is nothing else than the application of knowledge to a given act. But knowledge is in the reason. A will therefore at variance with an erroneous reason is against conscience.
I-II, q. 19, a. 5, §4.

They say that if conscience tells us to do anything which is good of its kind, there is no error.
I-II, q. 19, a. 5.

CONSENT

Consent implies a judgment on that which is consented to.
I-II, q. 74, a. 7.

CONSEQUENT

Consequents derive necessity from their antecedents.
I. q. 19, a. 8, §3.

CONSTITUTION

Some from their physical constitution have stronger inclinations than others.
II-II, q. 155, a. 4, §2.

CONSTITUTIVE

Good and evil are constitutive differences in moral matters.
I, q. 48, a. 1, §2.

CONSTRAINT

The necessity of constraint, as being contrary to the will, causes sadness.
II-II, q. 88, a. 6, §2.

CONTEMNING

No one ought to contemn another, or do him any hurt, without cogent reason.
II-II, q. 60, a. 4.

CONTEMPLATING

The contemplating life is better than the active, becoming a man in respect of the most excellent element in his nature, namely, his understanding. It is more self-sufficient and needs fewer things, and is loved for its own sake, while the active life is directed to something ulterior to itself.
II-II, q. 182, a. 1.

CONTEMPLATION

By works of contemplation, man soars higher above sensible things.
II-II, q. 168, a. 2.

The pleasure of contemplation has no sorrow annexed to it.
I-II, q. 35, a. 5.

One takes pleasure in contemplation or discussion.
I-II, q. 33, a. 3.

Contemplation is especially sought after for its own sake.
I-II, q. 3, a. 5.

Others have naturally a purity and peace of soul fitting them

for contemplation; and if these persons are totally set aside for active occupations, they will suffer loss.
II-II, q. 182, a. 4.

Men who wish to give themselves to contemplation must withdraw themselves more than other men from fleshly desires.
II-II, q. 142, a. 1.

CONTEMPLATIVE
The goods of the contemplative life are better than the goods of the active life.
II-II, q. 152, a. 2.

The name of contemplatives is bestowed, not simply on persons who contemplate, but on such as devote their whole lives to contemplation.
II-II, q. 81, a. 1.

CONTENTION
Contention—when one wrangles in words clamorously with another.
II-II, q. 132, a. 5.

CONTINENCE
Continence is a perfection of the rational faculty, holding out against passion so as not to be carried away.
I-II, q. 58, a. 3, §2.

The name continence is taken in two ways. Some authors take the name to mean abstinence from all sexual pleasure. But others call continence resistance to evil passions in cases where they are violent.
II-II, q. 155, a. 1.

CONTINGENCY
Some things are contingent.
I, q. 22, a. 4.

The acts of man, being subject to free choice, are contingent.
1, q. 14, a. 13.

CONTRADICTION
Whatever implies a contradiction cannot form a word or a concept.
I, q. 25, a. 3.

Contradictions are beyond the scope of the divine omnipotence.
I, q. 25, a. 4.

CONTRADICTION, LAW OF
The first principle requiring no proof is this, that there is no

affirming and denying of the same thing at the same time.
I-II, q. 94, a. 2.

CONTRADICTION, SPIRIT OF
Who is possessed with the spirit of contradiction, going to excess in annoyance, sins more grievously than the complaisant man, or flatterer, who goes to excess in giving pleasure. In point of exterior motives, sometimes flattery is the graver sin, and sometimes the spirit of contradiction.
II-II, q. 116, a. 2.

CONTRARY
One contrary is taken away by another contrary supervening.
II-II, q. 24, a. 12.

Contrary is further removed from contrary than a simple negation of the thing, as black is further removed from white than simply not white.
II-II, q. 79, a. 4.

CONTUMELY
By the fact of speaking out against a man openly and to his face you seem to make light of him, and so to dishonor him; and therefore contumely wounds the honor of him against whom it is uttered.
II-II, q. 73, a. 1.

CONVENTION
Human convention belongs to positive law.
II-II, q. 66, a. 2, §1.

CONVERSION, SPIRITUAL
The turning of the indifferent towards God is called conversion to God.
I, q. 62, a. 3, §3.

CORRECTION
It is more difficult to bring back to the truth one who errs in a matter of principle; and in like manner in practical things, it is more difficult to bring back one who errs in respect of the goal and aim of life.
II-II, q. 156, a. 3, §2.

CORRECTION, FRATERNAL
Fraternal correction is an act of charity, more so than the cure of bodily infirmity, or the relief of exterior distress.
II-II, q. 33, a. 1.

Fraternal correction is directed to the amendment of our brother,

and therefore it falls under precept inasmuch as it is necessary to this end, but not so that an erring brother should be corrected in every place, or at every time.
II-II, q. 33, a. 2.

CORRUPTION
What is first in generation is last in corruption.
II-II, q. 162, a. 7.

COST
Great works cannot be without expenditure and cost.
II-II, q. 134, a. 3, §2.

COUNTRY
After God, man is most in debt to his parents and to his country.
II-II, q. 101, a. 1.

COVETOUSNESS
Covetousness is opposed to liberality; and in this way it involves an inordinate attachment to riches.
II-II, q. 118, a. 4.

The prudence of the covetous is not true prudence, which devises various ways and means of making money; and the same of the justice of the covetous, which scorns to touch others' possessions for fear of losing heavily thereby; and the same of the temperance of the covetous, by which they abstain from luxury as being an expensive taste; and the same of the fortitude of the covetous, with which, as Horace says, "they cross the sea, over the rocks and through the fire, to escape poverty."
II-II, q. 23, a. 7.

Covetousness is defined to be an immoderate love of having.
II-II, q. 118, a. 1.

COWARDICE
Cowardice flies from perils of death, for the avoidance of which the necessity of preserving life offers the greatest inducement.
II-II, q. 142, a. 3.

CRAVING
The craving after a good thing ought to be regulated according to reason: if it overpasses reason's rule, it must be vicious.
II-II, q. 131, a. 1, §1.

CREATION
To create is to form from nothing.
I, q. 45, a. 1.

36

Creation is the work of divine reason. . . . Causes cannot create but generate.
I, q. 45, a. 5.

Creation is without motion which characterizes only matter and generation.
I, q. 45, a. 2, §3.

Being created, a creature cannot create; only reason can be uncreated or creative.
I, q. 45, a. 5, §3.

CREATION AND GENERATION
Creation by reason is superior to generation by causes.
I, q. 45, a. 1, §2. Vide Cause and Reason; Emanation.

Augustine differentiates between the work of propagation or generation, which emanates from the nature, and the work of creation, which emanates from the spirit.
I, q. 45, a. 8.

CREATOR
The spiritual creator can produce value ideas out of nothing.
I, q. 75, a. 6, §2.

CREATURE
The rational creature knows and loves God.
I, q. 8, a. 3.

CREATURE, IRRATIONAL
Irrational creatures are not partakers in human reason, nor do they obey it.
I-II, q. 93, a. 5, §2.

Irrational creatures cannot share in human life, which is according to reason: here there can be no friendship with irrational creatures except perhaps metaphorically.
II-II, q. 25, a. 3.

CREED
Creed refers to God.
I, q. 1, a. 7.

CRIME
To a crime a remedy is applied by a penalty, which it is the judge's office to inflict.
II-II, q. 62, a. 3.

CRUELTY
Because cruelty means excess in the exaction of penalties, cruelty

is more directly opposed to clemency than to mercy.
II-II, q. 159, a. 1, §2.

CULPRIT

Before the culprit is condemned by the judge, he is not bound to restore more than he has taken; but after he is condemned, he is bound to pay the penalty.
II-II, q. 62, a. 3.

CURIOSITY

When one is eager to learn from an unlawful source, as in those who inquire of evil spirits about things to come: this is superstitious curiosity.
II-II, q. 167, a. 1.

CURSE

By cursing we understand the denouncing of another, by way either of command or wish.
II-II, q. 76, a. 3.

CUSTOM

Custom, especially that which is from the beginning, takes the place of nature.
C.G. I, 11, §1.

It is difficult to set aside the custom of the multitude.
I-II, q. 97, a. 3, §2.

When a thing is done many times over, it seems to come of the deliberate judgment of the reason. And in this way custom at once has the force of law, and abolishes law, and is the interpreter of the laws.
I-II, q. 97, a. 3.

What is customary becomes pleasant by becoming natural, for custom is a second nature.
I-II, q. 32, a. 2.

D

DAMNATION

God does not will the damnation of any one under the precise view of damnation, nor the death of any one inasmuch as it is death, but He wishes these things under the aspect of justice.
I-II, q. 19, a. 10, §2.

DANGER

The greatest dangers are the dangers of death.
II-II, q. 123, a. 5.

Dangers of death from sickess, or from a storm at sea, or from an attack of brigands, or other such cause, do not seem to threaten a man, in direct consequence of his pursuit of good, as do dangers of death in war, which are imminent directly in consequence of his just defense of the public good.
II-II, q. 123, a. 5.

DANGEROUS

If any man be dangerous to the community, and be corrupting it by any sin, the killing of him for the common good is praiseworthy.
II-II, q. 64, a. 2.

DARING

Fiery daring is a passion.
II-II, q. 127, a. 1.

DAY

There is no day without light.
I, q. 67, a. 4.

DEATH

Every man naturally shrinks from death.
I-II, q. 5, a. 3.

The danger of death is most difficult to face.
II-II, q. 136, a. 4, §1.

The most terrible of all bodily evils is death, that takes away all
the goods of the body.
II-II, q. 123, a. 4.

The suffering of death is not praiseworthy in itself but only
inasmuch as it is directed to some good and consisting in an
act of virtue.
II-II, q. 124, a. 3.

The extremest and most terrible of the evils of this life is death;
and therefore to compass one's own death in order to avoid
the other miseries of this life, is to take the greater evil to
escape the less.
II-II, q. 64, a. 5, §3.

DEBT
Sometimes one man takes upon himself another man's debt.
I-II, q. 87, a. 7.

That debt is legally due, which a man is bound by law to pay:
debts of this kind are the proper object of justice. That debt is
morally due, which one owes as part of the seemliness of virtue.
II-II, q. 80, a. 1.

Though liberality supposes not any legal debt, as justice does,
still it supposes a certain moral debt, considering what is becoming in the person himself who practises the virtue.
II-II, q. 117, a. 5, §1.

DECALOGUE
The commandments of the decalogue contain precisely the
intention of the lawgiver, who is God.
I-II, q. 100, a. 8.

All the commandments of the decalogue are directed to the
love of God and of our neighbor; and therefore the precepts
of charity needed not to be enumerated among the commandments of the decalogue, but are included in them all.
II-II, q. 44, a. 1, §3.

DECEIT
There are two ways of deceiving in word and deed. One way is
by telling lies and breaking promises. In another way one may
be deceived by the fact that we do not open our purpose or
declare our mind.
II-II, q. 40, a. 3.

The desire to deceive goes to make the lie perfect, but does not enter into its specific essence.
II-II, q. 110, a. 1, §3.

DECEPTION
Deception often creeps in accidentally.
I, q. 58, a. 5.

DECLARATION
Proper object of any declaration or assertion is truth or falsehood.
II-II, q. 110, a. 1.

Though dumb animals give certain declarations or indications, yet they do not intend to indicate or declare anything; but they do some action by natural instinct, and on that instinct declaration ensues.
II-II, q. 110, a. 1.

DECORUM
As regards bodily movements and actions, the check of moderation is imposed by decorum.
II-II, q. 143, a. 1.

DEFECT
Defects are overcome by perfection.
I, q. 21, a. 3.

Defects are found in nature less than in man.
I, q. 49, a. 3, §5.
What is mingled with anything else suffers a defect in kind.
II-II, q. 77, a. 2.

DEFENDANT
An accused is not bound to confess the whole truth, but that only which the judge can ask and ought to ask of him according to the order of law.
II-II, q. 69, a. 2.

DEFICIENCY
Useful things are sought after for the supplying of some deficiency.
II-II, q. 129, a. 3, §5.

DEFILEMENT
The body is not defiled except by the consent of the mind.
II-II, q. 64, a. 5, §3.

DEFINITION
A definition contains genus and difference.
I, q. 3, a. 5.

An essence is expressed by a definition.
I, q. 29, a. 2, §3.

The right definition of one is false of another.
l. q. 17, a. 3.

An effect is not defined by the relation to its cause.
I, q. 44, a. 1, §1.

DEGENERATION

The will of man may alter so as to degenerate from the virtue, the exercise of which is the principal element of happiness.
I-II, q. 5, a. 4.

DELIBERATION

Deliberation of the reason is the proper principle of human actions.
I-II, q. 1, a. 1, §3.

Art would be impeded in its action, if it had to deliberate about the thing to be done when it ought to be doing it.
II-II, q. 158, a. 1, §2.

DELICIOUSNESS

To every taste deliciousness is pleasant, but to some men most pleasant is the deliciousness of wine, to others the deliciousness of honey, and so of the rest.
I-II, q. 1, a. 7.

DELIGHT

There are two sorts of delight: one physical, following upon bodily contact; another psychical, following the soul's apprehension.
II-II, q. 123, a. 8.

Because bodily delights are better known, they have arrogated to themselves the name of pleasure.
I-II, q. 2, a. 6.

The desire of good and the desire of delight stand on the same footing, delight being nothing else than the repose of desire in good.
I-II, q. 2, a. 6, §1.

The vehemence of the desire of sensible delight arises from the operations of the senses being more readily perceptible, as being the beginnings of our knowledge: hence also sensible delights are gone after by the greater number of men.
I-II, q. 2, a. 6, §2.

If any man were so far to shun delight as to omit what was

necessary for the maintenance of nature, he would sin as going
against the natural order.
II-II, q. 142, a. 1.

DELUGE
God removed man by deluge whom He had previously created.
I, q. 10, a. 7, §1.

DEMOCRITUS
Democritus and almost all ancient philosophers did not differen-
tiate between intellect and sense (spirit and matter).
I, q. 84, a. 6.

DENOUNCER
A denouncer does not bind himself to proof: hence neither is he
punished, if he fail to prove what he has said.
II-II, q. 68, a. 2, §3.

DENUNCIATION
This is the difference between denunciation and accusation, that
in denunciation the object is the amendment of a brother, but in
accusation the punishment of a crime.
II-II, q. 68, a. 1.

DEPOSIT
When a man hands over the thing that is his, making it return-
able to himself, and bargaining that the receiver shall not use it
in the meanwhile, but shall merely hold it in safe-keeping, it is
called deposit or a pledge.
II-II, q. 61, a. 3.

DESIRABLE
To see, to live, and to understand, is something desirable and
lovely to all.
II-II, q. 34, a. 1.

DESIRE
Desires of food and sex are ordained to the maintenance of
nature.
II-II, q. 142, a. 2, §2.

Desire intends only the good or the apparently good.
I, q. 63, a. 1.

All things that a man desires are desired for the sake of the last
end. Whatever a man desires, he desires in the light of a good
thing.
I-II, q. 1, a. 6.

DESPAIR

Despair follows on fear, for the reason of a person's despairing is his fear of the difficulty which attaches to what is in itself a good to hope for.
I-II, q. 45, a. 2.

The movement of despair, which is formed upon a false estimate of God, is sinful.
II-II, q. 20, a. 1.

DETERMINATION

Every material being is determined, but the divine or spiritual being is undetermined.
I, q. 19, a. 4. Vide Free Choice

DETRACTION

The essential purpose of detraction is the blackening of another's character.
II-II, q. 73, a. 2.

DETRACTOR

A detractor is so called, not as diminishing aught of the truth, but as diminishing his neighbor's good name.
II-II, q. 73, a. 1, §1.

DEVIL

The devil, who aims at the perdition of mankind though he sometimes tells the truth, intends by these his answers to accustom men to give him credence, and thus he seeks to lure them on to something prejudicial to their salvation.
II-II, q. 95, a. 4.

DEVOTION

Devotion is an act of religion.
II-II, q. 82, a. 2.

Devotion ordinarily and in the first place causes spiritual joy in the mind, but consequently and incidentally it causes sorrow.
II-II, q. 82, a. 4.

Devotion is so called from devoting: hence they are called devoted, who in some manner devote themselves to God, so as to make themselves entirely subject to Him.
II-II, q. 82, a. 1.

DIFFERENCE

There is a qualitative and a quantitative difference of things.
I, q. 47, a. 2.

DIFFERENTIA SPECIFICA

The differentia specifica completes a definition.
I, q. 29, a 1, §4.

DIGNITY

In the dignity of his person, a neighbor is injured secretly by detraction.
II-II, q. 41, a. 3.

DIONYSIUS

Dionysius declares that spiritual values cannot be comprehended through corporeal things.
I, q. 88, a. 2.

DISAGREEMENT

Disagreement over small matters counts for no disagreement at all.
II-II, q. 29, a. 3, §2.

DISCIPLINE

With the young discipline goes further.
I-II, q. 95, a. 1.

One man must receive from another training and discipline whereby virtue is arrived at.
I-II, q. 95, a. 1.

To render discipline to one willing to receive it, is lawful to any man. But to apply discipline to an unwilling subject, belongs to him alone who has another entrusted to his charge.
II-II, q. 65, a. 2, §3.

DISCORD

Discord—when one will not give up his own will to live at peace with others.
II-II, q. 132, a. 5.

To raise a discord to the destruction of evil concord is praiseworthy.
I, q. 58, a. 3, §1.

Discord means a jarring of wills, inasmuch as the will of one party is set on one thing, and the will of another on another.
II-II, q. 37, a. 1, §2.

DISCURSIVENESS

Discursive knowledge is the result of other knowledge.
I. q. 58, a. 3, §1.

There would be no discursiveness of reasoning, if man would know at once all conclusions of a known principle.
I, q. 58, a. 3.

DISEASE

A wise physician suffers his patient to fall into a disease of milder type for the cure of a more grievous malady.
II-II q. 162, a. 6, $.

DISOBEDIENCE

Disobedience—when one refuses to fulfil a superior's command.
II-II, q. 132, a. 5.

DISPARAGEMENT

You are not always bound to resist disparagement by charging it with falsehood, especially if you know that what is said is true.
II-II, q. 73, a. 4, §2.

DISPENSATION

If it is ruled absolutely that a vow is not to be observed, that is called a dispensation from the vow.
II-II, q. 88, a. 10.

A dispensation properly means a measuring out to individuals of something held in common. Hence the ruler of a household is called a dispenser, inasmuch as he allots to every one of the household in due weight and measure both duties and the necessaries of life.
I-II, q. 97, a. 4.

DISPOSITION

A certain sweetness of disposition moves one to abhor all that can give pain to another.
II-II, q. 157, a. 3.

DISSENT

Dissent, which is the proper act of unbelief, is an act of the intellect, as also is assent, an act of the intellect moved by the will.
II-II, q. 10, a. 2.

DISTINCTION

A sinner is not naturally distinguishable from just men; and therefore he needs a public judgment to make him out.
II-II, q. 64, a. 3, §2.

DISTRESS

Psychical distress is overcome by the delight of virtue.
II-II, q. 123, a. 8.

If a need be so plain and pressing, that clearly the urgent necessity has to be relieved from whatever comes to hand, then the

man may lawfully relieve his distress out of the property of another.
II-II, q. 66, a. 7.

DIVINATION

By the name of divination is understood some sort of prediction of things to come. Now things to come may be predicted in two ways: one way in their causes; in another way in themselves.
II-II, q. 95, a. 1.

Then only is a man said to divine, when he arrogates to himself in an undue manner the foretelling of future events; and this is certainly a sin.
II-II, q. 95, a. 1.

DOCTOR

A doctor can more accurately predict the course of a sickness the more profoundly he knows its causes.
I, q. 57, a. 3.

DOING

What we can do with the aid of friends, we can in a certain manner do by ourselves.
I-II, q. 5, a. 5, §1.

DOUBT

Some acts of the intellect involve thinking without firm assent, without inclining to either side, as in doubt.
II-II, q. 2, a. 1.

DREAM

Divine revelation is more clearly conceived in a dream, or in a state of suspended senses.
I, q. 12, a. 11.

DRESS

The wearing of a mean dress is particularly proper in those who exhort other men by word and example to penance.
II-II, q. 169, a. 1, §2.

DRINK

When one drinks a great quantity by medical advice for the purposes of an emetic, the drink so taken is not to be considered to be in excess.
II-II, q. 150, a. 2, §3.

DRUNKARD

A drunken man may sometimes utter words that signify profound ideas, which however his mind is quite incapable of appreciating.

I-II, q. 77, a. 2, §5.

Drunkards have their use of reason fettered or impeded.

I-II, q. 33, a. 3.

DRUNKENNESS

Drunkenness, meaning the mere loss of reason that comes of drinking much wine, does not denote any guilt, but a penal loss consequent on guilt.

II-II, q. 150, a. 1.

DRY

Dry bodies receive with difficulty, but retain easily.

I, q. 78, a. 4.

DUALISM

Corporeal and spiritual things cannot have the same essence.

I, q. 50, a. 2.

The soul is entirely different from the body, if the essence of each is considered separately.

I, q. 76, a. 7, §3.

The dependence of the intellect on the body does not disprove the existence and the spirituality of the intellect.

I, q. 75, a. 2, §3.

The body is necessary for intelligent action, but is not an organ of the intellect.

I, q. 75, a. 2, §3.

The body is not an attribute of the soul (life) although the soul (life) is united to the body.

I, q. 75, a. 7, §3.

Varro maintained that man is neither soul alone, nor body alone, but both soul and body.

I, q. 75, a. 4.

DUE

To a man is due what is his own.

I, q. 21, a. 1, §3.

DULNESS

Dulness of perception in intellectual things is put down as a daughter of gluttony.

II-II, q. 148, a. 6.

DUTY

A thing is due in two ways, for its own sake or for the sake of something else.

II-II, q. 44, a. 1.

E

EATING

Eating is an animal function.
I, q. 51, a. 3.

Eating implies food taken and converted into the body of the eater.
I, q. 51, a. 3, §5.

ECLIPSE

The astronomers know from computation of the heavenly movements that eclipses will happen.
I, q. 57, a. 2.

ECONOMICAL

The pettily economical man diligently applies himself to accounts, because he has an inordinate fear of wasting his goods even in the least things.
II-II, q. 135, 1, 2.

The pettily economical man primarily intends the smallness of his expense, and consequently the paltriness of his work, an effect which he does not stick at, so that he can make the expense small.
II-II, q. 135, a. 1.

ECONOMY

Petty economy is a vice.
II-II, q. 135, a. 1.

EDUCATION

It is manifest that for the education of man there is required, not only the care of the mother by whom he is nourished, but much more the care of the father, by whom he has to be trained and defended.
II-II, q. 154, a. 2.

EFFECT

An effect cannot reach beyond its cause.
C.G. I, 43, §8.

An effect points to its cause.
I, q. 32, a. 1.

EFFORT

A greater earnestness of effort is applied where there is fear of a failure.
II-II, q. 55, a. 6.

A man makes no effort on points in which he is very wanting.
II-II, q. 36, a. 1.

It is by human effort that man is rendered the bondsman either of justice or of sin.
II-II, q. 183, a. 4.

EGG

One egg is not the image of another, not being copied from it.
I, q. 35, a. 1.

ELECTION

Election implies love.
I, q. 23, a. 4.

As intention is of the end, so election is of the means. Thus election is always of human acts.
I-II, q. 13, a. 4.

EMANATION

We must consider not only the emanation of a material effect from a material cause, but also the emanation of a spiritual consequence from a spiritual reason, which is God; and the spiritual emanation is called creation. **Vide** Creation.
I, q. 45, a. 1.

EMBRYO

The embryo has only a sensitive soul.
I, q. 76, a. 3, §3.

EMETIC

It is not necessary for the drink to be intoxicating to act as an emetic, because even warm water will serve the purpose: and therefore this would furnish no excuse for drunkenness.
II-II, q. 150, a. 2, §3.

EMULATION

We may be saddened at another's good, not because he has the

good, but because the good that he has is wanting to us; and this is properly emulation.
II-II, q. 36, a. 2.

END

The end has the preference over the means to the end.
II-II, q. 104, a. 3.

END, LAST

If there were no last end, nothing would be desired, nor any action have a term, nor would the intention of the agent rest.
I-II, q. 1, a. 4.

It is impossible for the will of one man at the same time to go out to several diverse objects as to so many different last ends.
I-II, q. 1, a. 5.

ENDOWMENT

Men sometimes attribute to themselves lower endowments, by reticence of the higher endowments that are in them, and unfolding and bringing out as their own certain lesser endowments, which however they recognize to be in their possession.
II-II, q. 113, a. 1.

ENDURANCE

Endurance is more difficult than taking the offensive.
II-II, q. 123, A. 6, 1.

The principal act of fortitude is endurance, or the remaining steady and unflinching in dangers, rather than attacking.
II-II, q. 123, a. 6.

Endurance takes a long time; but one may attack by a sudden movement.
I/-II, q. 123, a. 6, §1.

ENEMY

A man must be prepared even in a special manner to love his enemy and aid him in the hour of need, or if he should ask pardon.
II-II, q. 83, a. 8.

Our preparations to attack our enemies are to be hidden from them. Such concealment belongs to the nature of stratagems.
II-II, q. 40, a. 3.

The love of enemies is a necessary point of charity, to the effect that a man loving God and his neighbor should not exclude his enemies from the general compass of his love of his neighbor.
II-II, q. 25, a. 8.

The fact that enemies are our enemies ought to displease us. But they are not contrary to us inasmuch as they are men, capable of happiness; and in that respect we are bound to love them.
II-II, q. 25, a. 8, §2.

ENTIRENESS
Entireness was to be specified in laying down the precept of the love of God.
II-II, q. 44, a. 4.

ENUNCIATION
The intellect is capable of forming enunciations.
I, q. 14, a. 14.

ENVY
Envy is a sadness at another's good.
II-II, q. 36, a. 2.

Those who seek pre-eminence are moved against men of seeming eminence as being hindrances to their pre-eminence; and this is the zeal of envy.
I-II, q. 28, a. 4.

A man makes no effort on points in which he is very wanting: and therefore he feels no envy when any one excels him therein.
II-II, q. 36, a. 1.

The mere mention of envy points at once to something evil.
II-II, q. 158, a. 1.

EQUALITY
Equality is a relation of one thing to another.
II-II, q. 57, a. 1.

EQUITY
Equity is a kind of higher rule of human acts.
II-II, q. 120, a. 1, §1.

Equity in some sort is contained under legal justice, and in some sort goes beyond it.
II.II, q. 120, a. 2, §1.

Equity does not abandon justice absolutely, but only justice as fixed by law. Nor is it opposed to that severity, which abides by the words of the law in cases where it is proper to abide by them: to abide by them otherwise is an error.
II-II, q. 120, a. 1, §.

EQUIVOCATION
The same word applied in different senses, or to different things,
is an equivocation.
I, q. 3, a. 5.

ERECT
The erect stature befits man.
I, q. 91, a. 3, §3.

ERROR
A man easily errs in word.
II-II, q. 89, a. 2.

In speculative matters he who errs in principle is beyond the
reach of persuasion; but he who errs indeed, but adheres to
first principles, may be recalled by the aid of those same principles. And so in matters of conduct.
I-II, q. 72, a. 5.

ESSENCE
The essence is included in the definition.
II-II, q. 58, a. 6.

ESSENTIAL
All things that bear the name of 'essential,' contain no admixture
of any foreign element.
C.G. - I, 39, §1.

ESTIMATE
An estimate of human goods should not be taken by the judgment of fools, but by that of wise men, as an estimate of pal-
atable and unpalatable food is taken by the judgment of those
whose sense of taste is in good order.
I-II, q. 2, a. 1, §.

Our estimates of things must not be made simply by the ruling
of the sensitive appetite, but rather by the ruling of the intellectual appetite.
I-II, q. 4, a. 2, §2.

ETERNITY
We know eternity by way of time.
I, q. 10, a. 1.

ETHICS
Plato, wishing to save the validity of spiritual science (ethics),
asserted that there are, besides physical phenomena (apprehended in natural science), spiritual values, which he called
value ideas, by participation or belief in which a man becomes

a moral person. Accordingly, spiritual science does not deal with material things, but with immaterial, peculiar moral ideas.
I, q. 84, a. 1. Vide Participation.

EVIDENCE
Sometimes a man's evidence is called for, sometimes not.
II-II, q. 70, a. 1.

EVIL
Worse is an evil man than a beast, and more noxious, as the Philosopher says.
II-II, q. 64, a. 2, §3.

Evil must not be done that good may come of it.
II-II, q. 64, a. 5, §3.

There is a reason behind every evil.
I, q. 49, a. 1.

The thought of evil often augments the inclination towards evil.
I, q. 22, a. 3, §3.

The wise man chooses a lesser evil in order to avoid a greater one.
I, q. 48, a. 6.

Evils render things worse.
I, q. 19, a. 9.

In this life all evil cannot be excluded. The present life is liable to many evils that cannot be avoided, ignorance on the part of the intellect, inordinate affection on the part of the desire, and manifold penal inflictions on the part of the body.
I-II, q. 5, a. 3.

God permits some evils lest the good things should be obstructed.
I, q. 23, a. 5, §3. Vide Theodicy.

Evil is never loved except under an aspect of good, inasmuch as it is good in a restricted sense.
I-II, q. 27, a. 1, §1.

EVIL-DOER
The slaying of an evil-doer is lawful inasmuch as it is directed to the welfare of the whole community, and therefore appertains to him alone who has the charge of the preservation of the community.
II-II, q. 64, a. 3.

EXCELLENCE
One way of trying to show forth one's excellence is indirectly,

by showing that you are not inferior to any one else.
II-II, q. 132, a. 5.

A comparison of superior excellence has no place among persons on the side on which they agree, but on the side on which they differ.
II-II, q. 184, a. 8.

A man's excellence is taken to obtain especially in point of happiness.
I-II, q. 2, a. 2.

To God a singular excellence attaches, inasmuch as He infinitely transcends all things in every manner of excellence.
II-II, q. 81, a. 4.

EXCESS
The golden mean of reason may be spoiled by excess.
II-II, q. 126, a. 2.

Excess is attributable to him who blurts out his own doings and feelings unseasonably; and defect to him who conceals them when he ought to declare them.
II-II, q. 109, a. 1, §3.

When one eats or drinks a great quantity by medical advice for the purposes of an emetic, the food or drink so taken is not to be considered to be in excess.
II-II, q. 150, a. 2, §3.

There is no difficulty in there being several excesses in different respects to one golden mean.
II-II, q. 131, a. 2, §1.

EXCHANGE
In exchanges we must equalize thing to thing, so that whatever excess one party gets, over and above what is his own, of what belongs to another, so much exactly he should restore to the party to whom it belongs.
II-II, q. 61, a. 2.

Exchange is twofold: either an exchange in kind, of commodity for commodity, or an exchange of a commodity for money, but in any case having for motive the necessity of living.
II-II, q. 77, a. 4.

EXECUTION
To execute a murderer is sometimes a good.
I, q. 19, a. 6.

The moving principle of the execution is that from whence the work begins.
I-II, q. 1, a. 4.

EXEMPLAR
An exemplar, that is, an exemplary commandment is identical with a value idea.
I, q. 44, a. 3.

EXEMPLAR, DIVINE
The divine being is the supreme exemplar of all religious things.
I, q. 44, a. 3.

EXEMPLAR, NORMATIVE
Value ideas are normative exemplars or directives existing in the divine mind.
I, q. 15, a. 3.

So far as the value idea is the principle of the judging of actions, it is called a normative exemplar or directive, belonging to practical wisdom.
I. q. 15, a. 3.

EXISTENCE
There are many sorts of existence: to be, to live, to sense, to understand.
I, q. 74, a. 4, §3.

Exerything is by its own existence.
C.G. I, 22, §2.

'Existence' denotes a certain actuality: for a thing is not said to 'be' for what it is potentially, but for what it is actually.
C.G. 1, 22, §4.

EXISTENCE, HUMAN
It is impossible that the last end of human reason and will should be the preservation of human existence.
I-II, q. 2, a. 5.

EXPEDIENCY
When we are bound to apply a remedy to evils, whether our own or other people's, it is expedient for the safer application of the remedy to suppose the worst side of the case.
II-II, q. 60, a. 4, §3.

EXPENSE
Great works cannot be done without great expenses.
II-II, q. 134, a. 3.

Expense means parting with money, from which a man may be restrained by excessive love of money.
II-II, a. 3.

EXPERIENCE

By experience a man acquires a faculty of doing a thing easily.
I-II, q. 50, a. 5.

Experience is essentially opposed to suspicion.
II-II, q. 60, a. 3.

Experience is a cause of hope, inasmuch as by experience a man gets the idea that something is possible to him which previously he counted impossible. But in this way experience may also be a cause of lack of hope, because, conversely, by experience a man is convinced that something is not possible to him which he used to think possible.
I-II, q. 50, a. 5.

EXTOLLING

A man extols himself by speaking of himself above what he is in truth and reality.
II-II, q. 112, a. 1.

A man should so extol the good of others as not to contemn the good gifts with which he himself is endowed: for at that rate these gifts would be rendered to him a matter of sadness.
II-II, q. 35, a. 1, §3.

EYE

The pupil of the eye is affected by the color.
I, q. 75, a. 3.

F

FACE
Man's face expresses his vital feelings.
I, q. 91, a. 4, §4.

FACULTY
Faculty signifies a power apt for action.
I, q. 83, a. 3, §2.

FAITH
Faith imports the assent of the intellect to that which is believed.
II-II, 1, a. 4.

Faith is of the spiritual values that are seen not, and hope is of the things that are possessed not.
I-II, q. 62, a. 3, §2.

Faith is a sort of knowledge . . . but falls short of it when knowledge is science.
I, q. 12, a. 13, §3. (Ed. note: Since knowledge always is science, faith never is knowledge of God, but faith in, or love of, God.)

FALL, SPIRITUAL
Nothing can become to a man a sufficient cause of sin, that is, of a spiritual fall, but his own will.
II-II, q. 43, a. 1, §3.

In the course of the spiritual way one is exposed to a spiritual fall by the deed or act of another, who by his advice or persuasion or example draws you to commit sin.
II-II, q. 43, a. 1.

FALSEHOOD
Suppression of truth is one thing; the putting forward of falsehood another.
II-II, q. 69, a. 2.

Falsehood is the evil of the intellect, as truth is its good.
I-II, q. 5, a. 4.

FALSITY

Falsity can be found in the same realm where truth exists.
I, q. 17, a. 1.

As truth implies an adequate comprehension of things, so falsity implies an inadequate comprehension of them.
I, q. 17, a. 4.

FASHION

Some ladies may be excused from sin, when their dressing is not done out of vanity, but in compliance with a fashion to the contrary of what has been laid down: though such a fashion is not praiseworthy.
II-II, q. 169, a. 2.

FASTING

Fasting is not acceptable to God except so far as it is the work of virtue.
II-II, q. 88, a. 2, §3.

Fasting is taken up that the mind may be more freely raised to the contemplation of spiritual values.
II-II, q. 147, a. 1.

FATHER

The father is not matched with his child as with something absolutely other than himself.
II-II, q. 57, a. 4.

FATIGUE

When the mind soars above the things of sense, and is intent upon the works of reason, the result is a certain psychical fatigue.
II-II, q. 168, a. 2.

As bodily fatigue is thrown off by rest of the body, so must psychical fatigue be thrown off by rest of the mind.
II-II, q. 168, a. 2.

FAULT

Fault being immoral has more the character of evil than amoral pain.
I, q. 48, a. 6.

Fault does not strive for punishment, as merit does for reward.
I, q. 48, a. 6, §1.

One ought not to incur any fault in doing good.
II-II, q. 104, a. 3, §3.

A good soul reckons it a fault, not only to fall short of common justice, which is really a fault, but also to fall short of the perfection of justice, which sometimes is not a fault.
I-II, q. 113, a. 1, §2.

What is faulty on one point may be useful on many others.
II-II, q. 77, a. 3, §2.

FAULT AND PAIN
One becomes immoral, not by pain, but by fault.
I, q. 48, a. 6.

FAVOR
A favor is a favor because it is bestowed gratuitously.
II-II, q. 106, a. 2.

FEAR
A man fears that by his doing what he ought to do the necessaries of life may come to fail him.
II-II, q. 55, a. 6.

Into them who do good works on a motive of love, fear is not to be breathed by punishments, but only into such as are not moved by love to good.
II-II, q. 108, a. 1, §3.

For a man to be afraid, there must be at hand some hope of safety.
I-II, q. 52, a. 2.

Fears lead to flight, and that is just what fortitude avoids.
II-II, p. 136, a. 4, §2.

It is harder to repress fear than to keep fiery daring without bounds.
II-II, q. 123, a. 6.

It is fear especially that diverts will from a difficult line of action; for fear means retirement before an evil fraught with difficulty.
II-II, q. 123, a. 3.

What is done through fear is done voluntarily, because the motion of the will is carried towards it, although not for the thing itself, but for the repelling of the evil that is feared.
I-II, q. 6, a. 4.

FEE
A man may justly take a fee for services that he is not bound to render.
II-II, q. 71, a. 4.

FEIGNED

A feigned faith draws the affection to that which is feigned about God, and separates it from the truth of God.
II-II, q. 44, a. 1.

FEVER

Phantasms appear in fever.
I, q. 84, a. 8, §2.

The tongue of a fever-stricken man tastes a sweet thing as being bitter.
I, q. 85, a. 6.

FIDELITY

Every violation of fidelity involves irreverence, but it is not every irreverence that contains a violation of fidelity.
II-II, q. 89, a. 8.

FIGHT

It is harder to fight with the stronger than with the weaker.
II-II, q. 123, a. 6, §1.

If a general orders his soldiers to fight, that soldier fulfils the precept perfectly, who fights and overcomes the enemy, according to the intention of his commander. He also fulfils it, though imperfectly, whose fighting does not lead to victory.
II-II, q. 44, a. 6.

FIGURE

Figure is terminated by a boundary.
I, q. 7, a. 3.

FINERY

Since women may lawfully adorn themselves, either to maintain the becoming level of their state, or even somewhat to improve upon it, and please their husbands, it follows that the makers of finery for this purpose do not sin in the practice of their art, except it be possibly by inventing sundry superfluous and curious novelties.
II-II, q. 169, a. 2, §4.

FIRE

The same fire acts more strongly on nearer than on more remote objects.
II-II, q. 27, a. 7.

FIRMNESS

Firmness has none of the praise of virtue if it be without moderation or rectitude or discretion.
I-II, q. 65, a. 1.

Firmness is required for the application of the mind to God: for the mind is applied to Him as to the final goal and first commandment; and such principles ought to be especially founded.
II-II, q. 81, a. 8.

FIRST AGENT
All reasons are determined by other reasons, except a first reason.
I, q. 69, a. 1, §2.

FISH
Certain fishes walk on land.
I, q. 71, a. 1.

FLABBINESS
For a man to put himself to death to escape penal inflictions, has indeed a certain appearance of fortitude, but it is not true fortitude: rather it is a sort of flabbiness of mind unable to endure penal ills.
II-II, q. 64, a. 5, §5.

FLABBINESS
Food and drink alike may hinder the good of reason, overwhelming it in excess of pleasure; and on that score abstinence is concerned alike with food and drink.
II-II, q. 149, a. 2, §1.

FLATTERY
The flatterer's praise sometimes becomes to the other an occasion of sin, even beside the intention of the flatterer.
II-II, q. 115, a. 2.

It will be a piece of flattery, if one will praise another on points he ought not to have praise, either because they are evil things, or because they are uncertainties.
II-II, q. 115, a. 1, §1.

FLAW
A flaw in a thing makes the thing here and now of less value than it appears.
II-II, q. 77, a. 3, §4.

FLESH
The flesh is for the soul, as the matter for the form, and the instrument for the principal agent.
II-II, q. 55, a. 1, §2.

FLYING
Man is unable to fly.
I, q. 62, a. 2, §2.

FOOD

Right reason does not make such a diminution of food as to render the man incapable of doing the work that is his duty.
II-II. q. 147, a. 1, §2.

No man ever desires unlimited meat or unlimited drink.
I-II, q. 30, a. 4.

FOOL

He who is strengthened by God, confesses that he is an utter fool according to human notions, because he despises the human things that the wisdom of men seeks after.
II-II, q. 113, a. 1, §1.

Also the fool is honored, who is set in place of God and in place of the whole community.
II-II, q. 63, a. 3.

FOOT

No part of the foot is a foot.
I, q. 3, a. 7.

FORECASTING

The intellect is able to forecast future events.
I, q. 86, a. 4.

FORGETFULNESS

Forgetfulness makes havoc of a man's learning.
I-II, q. 5, a. 4.

FORGIVENESS

It is false that God grants forgiveness to such as persist in sin, or bestows heavenly glory on them that abandon good works.
II-II, q. 21, a. 2.

FORNICATION

A person thinking about fornication may take delight in two things: in the thought itself, and in the fornication thought about.
I-II, q. 74, a. 8.

Fornication or adultery is a less sin than murder, and especially self-murder, which is the most grievous thing of all, because you harm yourself, whom you are most bound to love.
II-II, q. 64, a. 5, §3.

Simple fornication involves an inordinateness that tends to the hurt of the life of the child, who is to be born of such intercourse.
II-II, q. 154, a. 2.

FORNICATION, SPIRITUAL

In the spiritual union of the mind with certain objects there arises a delight, which is the matter of a spiritual chastity, metaphorically so called, or of a spiritual fornication, also metaphorically so called.

II-II, q. 151, a. 2.

FORTITUDE

It belongs to fortitude of mind, bravely to bear the infirmity of the flesh.

II-II, q. 123, a. 1, §1.

Fortitude deals principally with fears of things difficult, which may divert the will from the following of reason. And therefore fortitude deals with fears and ventures, repressing fears and moderating ventures.

II-II, q. 123, a. 3.

The virtue of fortitude prevents the reason from being swallowed up in the pains of the body; and the psychical distress is overcome by the delight of virtue.

II-II, q. 123, a. 8.

It belongs to fortitude to face, not any adversity whatever, but that which is most difficult to face, namely, danger of death.

II-II, q. 136, a. 4, §1.

Fortitude is a disposition of the soul whereby it is strengthened in that it is according to reason against all manner of assaults of passion or toil of active labors.

I, q. 61, a. 4.

Fortitude having two acts, to endure and to attack, does not employ anger for the act of endurance,—that act is done by the mere force of reason; but for the act of attack. For this act anger is employed rather than other passions, because it is the part of anger to assault the vexatious object.

II-II, q. 123, a. 10, §3.

The men of fortitude, who face dangers according to the judgment of reason, in the beginning seem remiss, because it is not from passion but with deliberation that they address themselves to their duty: but in the hour of danger they meet with no unforeseen experience, but frequently find the difficulty less than they had anticipated; and therefore they hold to their way more steadily.

I-II, q. 45, a. 4.

FOX

It is not an evil of the fox to be sly.
I, q. 63, a. 4, §3.

FRAUD

Trickery and fraud are equivalent to a lie; and this is the meaning of a fraudulent defense.
II-II, q. 69, a. 2.

To use fraud to sell a thing above its just price is a downright sin, being the deceiving of another to his loss.
II-II, q. 77, a. 1.

FREE CHOICE

There is free choice, where there is intellect.
I, q. 59, a. 3.

Human works are subject to free choice.
I, q. 14, a. 13.

Free choice expresses human dignity.
I, q. 59, a. 3.

God has free choice.
I, q. 19, a. 10. (Ed. note: Freedom is thus sufficiently proven, and it belongs, not to man, but to God). Vide Determination.

FREE WILL

Man is master of his own acts by reason and will: hence free will is said to be a function of will and reason.
IIII, q. 1, a. 1.

FREEDOM

Freedom from sin is true freedom.
II-II, q. 183, a. 4.

He would be free who would be his own master.
I, q. 21, a. 1, §3.

Freedom from sin goes along with bondage of justice: because both by the one and the other the man tends to what becomes a man.
II-II, q. 183, a. 4.

There is a twofold freedom, one from sin and one from justice. It is the bondage of sin or of justice, when one is bent either upon evil by the habit of sin, or upon good by the habit of justice.
II-II, q. 183, a. 4.

FRIEND

A friend is better than honor.
II-II, q. 74, a. 2.

The company of friends makes for the well-being of happiness.
I-II, q. 4, a. 7.

Every man is naturally every man's friend with a certain general love.
II-II, q. 114, a. 1, §2.

He is properly called a friend, to whom we wish any good; and that we are said to desire which we wish for ourselves.
I-II, q. 26, a. 4, §1.

Friends are requisite for carrying out an enterprise.
I-II, q. 4, a. 1.

FRIENDLINESS

If one wishes to give pleasure by praising, thereby to console the person that he fail not in tribulation, or also that he may be eager to advance in good, this will be part of the virtue of friendliness.
II-II, q. 115, a. 1, §1.

FRIENDSHIP

Good-will is not sufficient for the being of friendship, but there is required a mutual affection, because a friend is a friend to a friend.
II-II, q. 23, a. 1.

Friendship between kinsmen is more stable; but other friendships may prevail over it in the proper matter of each friendship.
II-II, q. 26, a. 8.

Friendship makes identity in willing and willing not.
II-II, q. 104, a. 3.

A man ought to suffer corporal loss for his friend; and in so doing he loves himself the more on his spiritual and mental side, inasmuch as what he does is a point of the perfection of virtue, which is a good of the mind.
II-II, q. 26, a. 4, §2.

Not every love has the character of friendship, but only that love which is attended with good-will.
II-II, q. 23, a. 1.

What is loved with a love of friendship is loved absolutely and by itself; but what is loved with a love of desire is not loved absolutely and by itself, but is loved for another.
I-II, q. 26, a. 4.

There can be no friendship with irrational creatures.
II-II, q. 25, a. 3.

FULNESS

Fulness of being is of the essence of good.
I-II, q. 18, a. 1.

FUTURE

The future can be known to us through its present causes.
I, q. 86, a. 4.

Future things, being subject to time, are singular.
I q. 86, a. 4.

Future events can be known with accurate knowledge, because they are necessarily effected by causes.
I, q. 57, a. 3.

G

GAIN

Gain is the end of trade.

II-II, q. 77, a. 4.

He who has money has not yet got gain actually, but only virtually.

II-II, q. 62, a. 4, §1.

GAMES

In the matter of games and sports there can be a virtue.

II-II, q. 168, a. 2.

GENERAL

The general is the result of abstraction from the particulars.

I. q. 57, a. 2, §1.

The word *general* may be taken in two ways. One way is the way of logical predication, as animal is a general term with respect to man and horse. A thing is otherwise called general in the way of efficiency, as the sun in reference to all bodies that are illuminated or changed by its virtue.

II-II, q. 58, a. 6.

What is general must be identical in essence with the things about which it is general.

II-II, q. 58, a. 6.

GENERATION

Generation by sexual intercourse is natural to man because of his animal nature.

I, q. 98, a. 2.

The active power of generation characterizes the male sex.

I, q. 92, a. 1.

Generated from a semen, an animal must be born of small size.

I, q. 78, a. 2, §3.

Some living beings do not possess the power of generation, being
generated by other species.
I, p. 92, a. 1.

The generation of one thing causes the corruption of another.
I, q. 19, a. 9.

What is last to be generated is the first to decay.
II-II, q. 107, a. 2.

GENERATION, SPIRITUAL

Men who have taken up the office of contemplation, and of
transmitting to others by a sort of spiritual generation spiritual
good, do well in abstaining from many sources of pleasure, from
which others do well not to abstain.
II-II, q. 142, a. 1, §2.

GENUS

The genus belongs to the essence of the species, and is included
in the definition of the same.
II-II, q. 58, a. 6.

GEOMETER

A geometer with a little study acquires the knowledge of a conclusion which he has never before considered.
I-II, q. 65, a. 1.

So long as the geometrical demonstration is correct, it matters
not how the geometer stands in his appetitive faculty, whether
he be in joy or in anger.
I-II, q. 57, a. 3.

GEOMETRY

In the science of geometry, the conclusions are things materially
known; but the demonstrations by which the conclusions are
known, are the formal reason of the knowledge.
II-II, q. 1, a. 1.

GLAD

To be glad is to repose in some pleasant thing.
I, q. 59, a. 4, §2.

GLORY

Man may commendably seek his own glory for the advantage of
others.
II-II, q. 132, a. 1, §1.

Glory denotes brilliancy and lustre.
II-II, q. 142, a. 4.

The seeking after glory does not of itself imply anything vicious; but the seeking after empty or vain glory means vice.
II-II, q. 132, a. 1.

In the larger sense of the word glory consists in being known, not necessarily to many, but to a few, to one, even to oneself, where one regards one's own good qualities as worthy of praise.
II-II, q. 132, a. 1.

Properly by the name *glory* is denoted the coming of somebody's good qualities to the knowledge and approbation of many.
II-II, q. 132, a. 1.

Human glory is frequently fallacious.
I-II, q. 2, a. 3.

GLUTTONY

The vice of gluttony does not reside in the substance of the food, but in the appetite ill-regulated by reason.
II-II, q. 148, a. 1, §1.

In the commission of gluttony there is the pleasure of food.
I-II, q. 72, a. 2.

GOAL

The object of the will is some goal in the shape of good. Therefore all human actions must be for a goal.
I-II, q. 1, a. 1.

The goal always excels the way to the goal.
II-II, q. 152, a. 5.

The goal, though it is last in execution, is first in the intention of the agent, and in this way stands as a cause.
I-II, q. 1, a. 1, §1.

GOAL, ULTIMATE

It is not necessary for one to be always thinking of the ultimate goal in every desire and in every work; but the efficacy of the first intention, which is made in view of the ultimate goal, remains in every desire of everything, even without any actual thought of the ultimate goal.
I-II, q. 1, a. 6.

As regards that in which the character of the ultimate goal is found, all men do not agree in their ultimate goal.
I-II, q. 1, a. 7.

It is impossible for one man to have several ultimate goals not in harmony with one another.
I-II, q. 1, a. 5.

If there were only one soul enjoying God, it would be happy, without having any neighbor of love.
I-II, q. 4, a. 8, §3.

God alone can fill the heart of man.
I-II, q. 2, a. 8.

Natural reason dictates to man subjection to some higher power on account of the deficiencies which he experiences in himself, wherein he needs to be aided and guided by some one above himself: and whatever that higher power may be, that it is which amongst all men is called God.
II-II, q. 85, a. 1.

God is a first or supreme reason.
I, q. 83, a. 1, §3.

God being a first reason, is a first agent.
I. q. 3, a. 2.

Some have assumed that God is corporeal.
I, q. 2, a. 1, §2.

God is in the highest degree immaterial or spiritual.
I. q. 14, a. 1.

God signifies His essence by spiritual values.
I. q. 1, a. 10.

God is the supreme, self-subsisting, most intelligent, and perfect being or the highest spiritual value.
I, q. 29, a. 3, §1.

God has a rational essence, that is, not a cognitive, but a normative essence.
I, q. 29, a. 3, §4.

It is impossible that spiritual God be matter.
I, q. 3, a. 2.

In God there is no sensitive appetite.
I-III, q. 59, a. 5, §3.

There is no quantity, but only meaning in God.
I, q. 28, a. 4.

We know God only through material effects.
I, q. 86, a. 2, §1. (Ed. note: Is God not known rather through his spiritual emanations?)

God certainly is the cause of corporeal things as He is the reason of spiritual values.
I, q. 13, a. 2. (Ed. note: But God seems to be a reason only, and not also a cause.)

God alone is the creator of our souls.
II-II, q. 85, a. 2.

The divine being is the highest exemplary reason of all religious things.
I, q. 44, a. 3.

The essence of God cannot be seen through material but through spiritual things.
I, q. 12, a. 11.

We should comprehend God, not in terms of the body, but in terms of the spiritual value.
I, q. 27, a. 1.

Spiritual God is only metaphorically denoted by names referring to corporeal things.
I, q. 10, a. 1, §4.

To see God by essence is above the nature, not only of man, but even of every creature.
I-II, q. 5, a. 5.

We shall see God, but without comprehending Him.
I, q. 86, a. 2, §1. (Ed. note: The seeing of the intellect is also comprehension.)

There are some points of intelligibility in God, accessible to human understanding, and other points that altogether transcend it.
C.G. I, 3, §1.

Though we cannot attain to God by sense, yet by sensible signs our mind is roused to tend to God.
II-II, q. 84, a. 2, §3.

God resides in the rational creature, that can know and love Him.
I, q. 8, a. 3.

There is a will in God.
I, q. 19, a. 1.

There are affirmative propositions about God.
I, q. 13, a. 12. (Ed. note: One thinks of God mostly in negative terms: He is immaterial, invisible, incorporeal, etc. But God is affirmatively or essentially spiritual.) **Vide** Name.

GOLDEN MEAN

The golden mean of virtue is taken, not according to quantity, but according to right reason.
II-II, q. 147, a. 1, §2.

The golden mean of reason may be spoiled by defect, as it may be spoiled by excess.
II-II, q. 126, a. 2.

The finding or the neglect of the golden mean of virtue in human acts and passions is a question of circumstances.
I-II, q. 7, a. 2, §3.

GOOD

Good is the reason of evil.
I, q. 49, a. 1, §1.

Among all creatures, the rational human creature mainly is destined for the good in the world.
I, q. 23, a. 7.

The public good is greater than the private good.
II-II, q. 42, a. 2.

The pursuit of some good should be man's motive for not shrinking from dangers of death.
II-II, q. 123, a. 5.

No bodily good apprehended by sense can be the perfect good of man, but is a trifle in comparison with the good of the soul.
I-II, q. 2, a. 6.

The good in respect to the senses differs from the good in respect to reason.
I, q. 49, a. 3, §5.

It is of the nature of good to be loved.
II-II, q. 34, a. 1.

That good must be most complete, which is pursued as his last end by him whose affections are best in order.
I-II, q. 1, a. 7.

Even the desire of a good thing needs to be duly regulated.
II-II, q. 167, a. 1, §2.

The knowledge of truth in itself is good; but it may be abused to an evil end, or inordinately desired.
II-II, q. 167, a. 1, §2.

The good of man consists in the knowledge of truth; but the sovereign good of man does not consist in the knowledge of any and every truth, but in the perfect knowledge of the highest truth.
II-II, q. 167, a. 1, §1.

GOOD, FINAL

Some seek riches as their complete and final good; others seek pleasure; others other things.
I-II, q. 1, a. 7.

GOOD, PERFECT
The perfect good is the ultimate goal.
I-II, q. 1, a. 6, §2.

GOOD, SPIRITUAL
The more we think of spiritual goods, the more pleasing they become to us.
II-II, q. 35, a. 1, §4.

The objects of bodily pleasure are corruptible and quickly fail; but the spiritual goods are incorruptible.
I-II, q. 31, a. 5.

GOOD, SUPREME
The more perfectly the supreme good is possessed, the more it is loved, and all things else despised. But with the desire of riches and all other temporal goods the contrary is the case; for when they are got, what is already in hand is despised, and something else desired, because their insufficiency is better recognized when they are possessed.
I-II, q. 2, a. 1, §3.

GOOD, UNIVERSAL
The object of the will is universal good.
I-II, q. 2, a. 8.

GOODNESS
Goodness supposes soundness all around, but any single defect makes an evil case.
II-II, q. 110, a. 3.

It belongs to goodness of soul to tend to the perfection of justice.
II-II, q. 113, 1, §2.

The goodness that is called truth is not truth in general, but a particular truth.
I, q. 16, a. 4, §3.

The truth is a kind of goodness.
I, q. 16, a. 4, §1.

There is a logical difference between goodness and truth.
I, q. 16, a. 4.

GOOD AND EVIL
Good and evil are predicated in relation to reason.
I-II, q. 18, a. 5.

As good things are sought more promptly for the pleasure that

attaches to them, so evil things are more vigorously avoided for sorrow and grief and pain.
I-II, q. 59, a. 3.

Good and evil in moral matters means agreement with or divergence from reason.
I-II, q. 34, a. 1.

GOOD AND TRUE
The good and the true are convertible.
I, q. 59, a. 2. Vide Goodness.

The good and the true, though differing logically, imply one another.
I, q. 87, a. 4, §3. (Ed. note: A logical difference is final.)

GOODS
Of all the goods of the present life man most loves life itself, and contrariwise most hates death.
II-II, q. 124, a. 3.

So long as his bodily life remains to a man, he has not yet shown in very deed his contempt of all the goods of the body.
II-II, q. 124, a. 4.

Temporal goods are subject to man that he may use them for his necessity, not that he may set up his rest in them, or be idly solicitous about them.
II-II, q. 55, a. 6, §1.

Temporal and material goods are indeed some good to man, but they are petty goods; the grand goods of man are spiritual.
I-II, q. 87, a. 7, §2.

GOODS, EXTERIOR
Exterior goods, subservient as they are to animal life, are not proper to the spiritual life.
I-II, q. 4, a. 7, §2.

All saleable articles may be had for money, but not spiritual goods: they cannot be sold.
I-II, q. 2, a. 1, §2.

GOODS, TEMPORAL
Temporal goods are not to be despised as instruments to aid us to the exercises of the fear and love of God.
II-II, q. 126, a. 1, §3.

Temporal goods cannot be simultaneously possessed by many.
II-II, q. 118, a. 1, §2.

GOSPEL

The Gospel law is a law of love.
II-II, q. 108, a. 1, §3.

GOVERNING

He who governs a family, may make regulations or standing orders, not however such as to have the character of law.
I-II, q. 90, a. 3, §3.

GOVERNMENT

For the benefit of society some of its members must be governed by wiser ones.
I, q. 92, a. 1, §2.

GRACE

There are some mortal sins that one can nowise avoid without grace.
I-II, q. 63, a. 2.

GRAMMAR

Grammar does not always make a man speak correctly, for a grammarian may use a barbarism.
I-II, q. 56, a. 3.

GRATITUDE

Where the favor is greater, there greater gratitude is requisite.
II-II, q. 106, a. 2.

GRAVITATION

Heavy bodies tend to the center of the world.
I, q. 28, a. 1.

GRIEF

When the soul is poured upon exterior things, then its attention is parted among them, and thus the inward grief is lessened.
I-II, q. 38, a. 2.

GROUND, ULTIMATE

God is the ultimate ground of all religious things.
I, q. 44, a. 4, §4.

GROWTH

An animal grows by the power of its soul.
I, q. 78, a. 2, §3.

The growing stage is generally to the end of the third seven years.
II-II, q. 147, a. 4, §2.

GUARDING

One can guard only what one knows.

I, q. 57, a. 2.

GUILT

The guilt of sin consists in a voluntary turning away from God.

II-II, q. 34, a. 2.

H

HABIT

A habit is a quality difficult to change.
I-II, q. 156, a. 3.

A habit not ony produces a readiness for well-doing, but also makes one use the readiness duly.
I-II, q. 56, a. 3.

By multiplication of acts there is generated a certain quality in the passive power that receives the impression, which quality is named a habit.
I-II, q. 51, a. 2.

HABIT, SPECULATIVE

Speculative habits are occupied with the quality of the things they consider, and not with the quality of the human appetite in regard of those things.
I-II, q. 57, a. 3.

HAND

The man, not the hand, acts.
I, q. 3, a. 8.

It is not properly said that the hand, but that the man with the hand strikes.
II-II, q. 58, a. 2.

HAPPINESS

Not all men wish for happiness.
I-II, q. 5, a. 8.

He is happy, who is sufficient for himself and wants nothing.
C.G I, 100, §4.

It is of the essence of happiness to be all in all by itself.
I-II, q. 2, a. 4.

Men is directed to happiness by interior principles, since he is directed to it by nature.
I-II. q. 2, a. 4.

Happiness is a perfect good, which entirely appeases the desire: otherwise it would not be the last end, if something still remained to be desired.
I-II, q. 2, a. 8.

It is impossible for the happiness of man to consist in riches, in fame or human glory, in power.
I-II, q. 2, a. 1, 3, 4.

It is impossible that happiness should consist in honor.
I-II, q. 2, a. 2.

Worldly happiness comprises wealth, pleasure, power, honor and fame.
I, q. 26, a. 4.

It is possible for some happiness to consist in the good use of power, which is by virtue, than in power itself.
I-II, q. 2, a. 4.

Happiness is the perfect good of man.
I-II, q. 2, a. 2.

Happiness is said to be the sovereign good of man, because it is the attainment or enjoyment of the sovereign good.
I-II, q. 3, a. 1, §2.

The goal most to be desired is happiness, the supreme goal of human life. And therefore the more anything partakes of the condition of happiness, the more it is to be desired.
II-II, 2, 118, a. 7.

Speaking of perfect happiness some have laid it down that no disposition of body is requisite for happiness: nay, that it is requisite thereto for the soul to be altogether separated from the body.
I-II, q. 4, a. 6.

Perfect happiness in the vision of God will either be in the soul without the body, or will be in a soul united to a body no longer animal but spiritual; and therefore in no way are exterior goods requisite for that happiness, bearing as they do upon animal life.
I-II, q. 4, a. 7.

Happiness itself, being a perfection of the soul, is a good inherent in the soul: but that in which happiness consists, or the object that makes one happy, is something outside the soul.
I-II, q. 7, §3.

Happiness consists rather in the activity of the speculative understanding than of the practical.
I-II, q. 3, a. 5.

The essence of happiness consists in an act of understanding. But the delight that follows upon happiness belongs to the will.
I-II, q. 3, a. 4.

Complete happiness consists in comprehending the highest spiritual value, namely, God.
I, q. 64, a. 2, §1.

HARM

A man sometimes knowingly and willingly does harm to himself, as in cases of suicide.
I-II, q. 73, a. 8, §2.

HARVEST

He who has sown seed in his land has not yet got the harvest actually, but only virtually.
II-II, q. 62, a. 4, §1.

HATRED

It is no excuse for a man that he hates another who hates him.
II-II, q. 108, a. 1.

To take delight in the evil of another belongs to hatred, which is repugnant to the charity with which we are bound to love all men.
II-II, q. 108, a. 1.

Hatred is a sort of dissonance of the appetite from that which is apprehended as unsuitable and hurtful.
I-II, q. 29, a. 1.

HEALTH

Health is desired for its contribution to life.
I, q. 87, a. 2, §3.

As what is the right measure for a man in health is often too much for a sick man, so also it may be that what is too much for a man in health is the right measure for one that is sick.
II-II, q. 150, a. 2, §3.

If we speak of human happiness such as can be had in this life, it is manifest that a good habit of body is requisite thereto of necessity; and that by ill-health of body man may be impeded in every virtuous activity.
I-II, q. 4, a. 6.

He is better disposed for health who can gain perfect health by the aid of medicine, than he who can get tolerably well without the aid of medicine.
I-II, q. 5, a. 5, §2.

HEART

The heart is the principle of animal life.
I, q. 75, a. 1.

HEAT

Heat is requisite for fire.
I-II, q. 4, a. 1.

HELP

In a certain case we should rather help a stranger, say, in extreme necessity, than even a parent not in such necessity.
II-II, q. 31, a. 3.

HERETIC

He who sins against the things of faith, is said to sin against God, as does the heretic, and the sacrilegious person, and the blasphemer.
I-II, q. 72, a. 4.

In a heretic who disbelieves one article of faith, no faith remains, either informed or uninformed.
II-II, q. 5, a. 3.

HIDE

Hide and hair are animal clothes.
I, q. 91, a. 3, §2.

HOLINESS

The name of holiness seems to denote two ideas, the one of purity, the other of firmness.
II-II, q. 81, a. 8.

Sometimes the less holy may be more available for the common good, by reason of worldly ability or business capacity.
II-II, q. 63, a. 2.

HOMICIDE

He who does not remove the conditions from which homicide follows, supposing it to be his duty to remove them, incurs in a manner the guilt of wilful homicide.
I-II, q. 64, a. 8.

Homicide is a more grievous sin if committed by a sober man than by a drunken man.
I-II, q. 76, a. 4, §2.

HONOR

Honor is understood to be the reward of virtue on the part of other men, who have nothing greater to bestow on the virtuous than honor.
II-II, q. 131, a. 1, §2.

Lovers of honor are more prone to envy.
II-II, q. 36, a. 1.

It must be observed that a person must be honored, not only for his own virtue, but also for the virtue of another: as rulers and clergymen are honored, though they be of evil life, inasmuch as they bear the person of God, and of the community over whom they are set.
II-II, q. 63, a. 3.

Honor is a testimony to the virtue of him who is honored; and therefore virtue alone is a due reason of honor.
II-II, q. 63, a. 3.

Those who despise honors in such a way as to do nothing unbecoming to gain them, and do not value them too highly, deserve praise.
II-II, q. 129, a. 1, §3.

Honor is paid to a person for some excellence of his, and so is a sign and testimony of that excellence which is in the person honored.
I-II, q. 2, a. 2.

Honor may indeed follow upon happiness, but happiness cannot consist principally in honor.
I-II, q. 2, a. 2.

Honor is due to God, and to beings of high excellence, as a testimony of preexistent excellence, not that the mere honor makes them excellent.
I-II, q. 2, a. 2, §2.

HOPE

The object of hope is good, difficult, but possible.
II-II, q. 21, a. 1.

One does not hope for what he cannot at all get; and in this hope differs from despair.
I-II, q. 50, a. 1.

The object of hope is future good, arduous, but possible of attainment.
I-II, q. 50, a. 5.

HORN

Horns and claws are the weapons of certain animals.
I, q. 91, a. 3, §2.

HORSE

A blind horse runs amuck; and the higher its speed, the more it hurts itself.
I-II, q. 58, a. 4, §3.

HORSE AND DONKEY
Horse and donkey are different beings, but both are animals.
I, q. 29, a. 4, §4.

HOUSE
Wall and roof are comprehended in the species of the house.
I, q. 12, a. 10, §1.

The constructed house is evidence of the architect's idea.
I, q. 93, a. 6.

An actual house is a house more truly than a potential house.
I, q. 18, a. 4, §3. (Ed. note: According to Kant 100 real coins and 100 imagined coins are 100 coins; the difference does not consist in the concept, but in the mode of existence. Indeed, "a physical house is like the house in the builder's mind." [I, q. 44, a. 3, §1].)

HUMAN
Those actions are properly called human, which proceed from a deliberate will. Any other actions attributed to man may indeed be styled actions of man, but not properly human actions, since they are not of man as he is a man.
I-II, q. 1, a. 1.

The human male and female are united for life; animals are not so closely associated.
I, q. 92, a. 2.

HUMANITY
A man is not the same as his humanity.
I, q. 3, a. 3.

HUMILITY
Humility makes man think little of himself in consideration of his own shortcomings. In like manner also magnanimity despises others inasmuch as they come short of the gifts of God: for it does not set such store to others as to do anything unbecoming for their sakes.
II-II, q. 129, a. 3, §4.

Humility honors others and accounts them superior beings, in so far as it discerns in them any of the gifts of God.
II-II, q. 129, a. 3, §4.

Humility checks the appetite, that it tend not to great things beyond right reason.
II-II, q. 161, a. 1, §3.

It is a point of humility that a man, from the consideration of his own defects, should abstain from extolling himself.
II-II, q. 35, a. 1, §3.

Humility particularly regards the subjection of man to God, for whose sake also he humbles himself in submission to the men.
II-II, q. 161, a. 1, §4.

HURT

To do hurt to another by work of hand is not without mortal sin.
II-II, q. 41, a. 1.

HYPOCRISY

By hypocrite is meant one who intends to counterfeit the holiness.
II-II, q. 111, a. 4.

Hypocrisy is simulation, not however any and every simulation, but only that by which a person pretends to a character not his own, as when a sinner pretends to the character of a just man.
II-II, q. 111, a. 2.

HYPOSTASIS

First principles are called hypostases.
I, q. 29, a. 1.

I

IDEA

The Greek word *idea* is in Latin *forma*.

I, q. 15, a. 1. (Ed. note: The adequate Latin term is opinio, that is, aestimatio rather than forma. At least the all-important Platonic ideas are essentially moral values or value ideas.)

Plato asserted that spiritual value ideas are the first object of science.

I, q. 88, a. 1. (Ed. note: Accordingly, natural phenomena are, though a secondary, a scientific object.)

Plato maintained that the objects of the understanding are also, and not exclusively, value ideas which are apprehended by participation rather than by abstraction. *Vide* Value Idea.

I, q. 85, a. 1. (Ed. note: Participating attention to spiritual values actually is identical with abstraction from physical phenomena.)

IDEALISM

There are spiritual values perfect in spiritual essence.

I, q. 51, a. 1.

IDOL

A Catholic and a pagan do not understand the same thing, when speaking of God. When the pagan says, *my idol is a God,* the Catholic replies, *your God is an idol.*

I, q. 13, a. 10, §5.

IDOLATRY

Heretics also have fallen into this error, saying that there is no danger in one externally worshipping idols, if he is seized in time of persecution, provided he keeps the faith in his heart.

II-II, q. 94, a. 2.

From the common heathen custom of worshipping all manner of creatures under certain images, the name of idolatry has been applied to any worship whatever of a creature, even if it be without images.

II-II, q. 94, a. 1, §3.

IGNORANCE

Ignorance is a privation of that knowledge that perfects the reason and hinders a sinful act, inasmuch as reason has the guidance of human acts.
I-II, q. 76, a. 1.

Ignorance has in it to cause involuntariness, as robbing the mind of knowledge, the necessary preliminary to a voluntary act.
I-II, q. 6, a. 8.

ILLUMINATION, SPIRITUAL

We call the increase of the intellectual understanding the illumination of the intellect.
I, q. 12, a. 5.

IMAGE

An image is made in the likeness of another thing, the original.
I, q. 35, a. 1, §1.

The movement of veneration to the image as such does not rest in it, but tends to that of which it is the image.
II-II, q. 81, a. 3, §3.

IMAGINATION

The imagination is a storehouse of sensible things received through the senses.
I, q. 78, a. 4.

IMMANENCE

The physical world, being internally determined by its own nature, apparently does not require any external government.
I, q. 103, a. 1.

IMPERFECTION

A man is imperfect, who is not what he ought to be.
I, q. 59, a. 3, §2.

IMPETRATION

Merit rests on justice, but impetration on favor.
II-II, q. 83, a. 16, §2.

IMPOSSIBLE

If we deny the impossible, we also tear down the necessary.
I, q. 25, a. 3.

IMPRISONMENT

To imprison any one, or otherwise detain him, is unlawful except it be done in course of justice, either as a punishment, or as a precaution for the avoidance of some evil.
II-II, q. 65, a. 3.

To lock a man up, or put him in fetters, belongs to him alone who has general control over the life and actions of another: because thereby the party is hindered, not only from doing evil, but also from doing good.

II-II, q. 65, a. 3, §3.

IMPULSE

Dumb animals and plants have no rational life, thereby to be led by themselves: but they are always led as it were of another, by natural impulse.

II-II, q. 64, a. 1, §2.

IMPURE

An impure heart is withdrawn from the love of God by the passion that inclines it to earthly things.

II-II, q. 44, a. 1.

IMPUTATION

Merit and demerit are imputed to rational men.

I, q. 22, a. 2, §5.

Sins are not imputed to people out of their senses.

II-II, q. 142, a. 3.

What a man does asleep, not having the free judgment of reason, is not imputed to him.

II-II, q. 154, a. 5.

INCEST

A most heinous sin is incest, which is against the natural reverence due to those who are bound to us by ties of kindred.

II-II, q. 154, a. 12.

INDETERMINISM

The divine being does not act from natural necessity, is therefore not naturally determined, but free.

I, q. 25, a. 25. **Vide Determination; Free Choice.**

The will of God has, in contradistinction to the will of man, no cause.

1, q. 19, a. 5.

INDICATION

Where no clear indications appear of another's wickedness, we ought to hold him to be good, putting a favorable construction on what is doubtful.

II-II, q. 60, a. 4.

INDIVIDUAL

Every individual stands to the whole community as the part to the whole.

II-II, q. 64, a. 2.

INEQUALITY

Inequality stems from perfection.

I, q. 47, a. 2, §3.

INFERIOR

Inferiors are subject to their superiors, not in all things, but in certain matters of limited range.

II-II, q. 104, a. 5, §2.

INFINITY

The understanding arrives at the concept of infinity through its contemplating successively one thing after another.

I, q. 86, a. 2.

The infinite in quantity relates only to matter (and not to spiritual God).

I, q. 7, a. 3, §4.

INFINITY, SPIRITUAL

The word *infinite* means without termination as regards matter, and immaterial as regards the value idea of God.

I-II, q. 7, a. 2.

INFLICTION, MEDICINAL

The mere necessity of the administration to human nature of medicinal inflictions arises from the corruption of nature.

I-II, q. 87, a. 7.

INFLUENCE

A thing can be influenced only by adequate things.

I, q. 63, a. 2.

It is harder not to be influenced by the present than by the future.

II-II, q. 123, a. 6, §1.

INGRATITUDE

It is a point of ingratitude in man, to contemn the good gifts that he has from God.

II-II, q. 35, a. 1, §3.

It belongs to the first degree of ingratitude that a man should render evil for good; to the second, that he should disparage the benefit he has received; to the third, that he should account the benefit an ill turn done him.

II-II, q. 107, a. 4.

INIQUITY

By iniquity man gains a certain good, pleasure, money, or the like.

I-II, q. 27, a. 1, §1.

INJURY

By having a bad opinion of another without sufficient cause, you do him an injury and condemn him.
II-II, q. 60, a. 4.

INJUSTICE

When a judge proceeds to condemn a man on suspicion: this is a direct act of injustice.
II-II, q. 60, a. 3.

INNOCENCE

It is nowise lawful to slay the innocent.
II-II, q. 64, a. 6.

In the state of innocence it would not be necessary to lead any one to advance in virtue by exercises that could be described as inflictions.
I-II, q. 87, a. 7.

INQUIRY

Diligent inquiry into others' doings sometimes makes for detraction.
II-II, q. 167, a. 2, §2.

INSENSIBILITY

It appears that insensibility to fear is a flaw in the character, caused it may be by want of love, or by elation of mind, or by stolidity, which last cause however excuses from sin, if it be invincible.
II-II, q. 126, a. 1.

As timidity is opposed to fortitude by excess of fear, the man fearing what he ought not: so insensibility in the matter of fear is opposed to fortitude by defect, a man not fearing what he ought to fear.
II-II, q. 126, a. 2.

INSTANT

The instant is indivisible.
I, q. 42, a. 2, §4.

INSTINCT

Dumb animals have a natural instinct, whereby they have movements interior and exterior to the movements of reason.
I-II, q. 46, a. 4, §2.

INSTRUCTION

Instruction presupposes knowledge.
I, q. 94, a. 3.

Instruction is for knowledge.
I-II, q. 4, a. 1.

INSTRUMENT

The instrument is for the principal agent.
II-II, q. 55, a. 1, §2.

Instruments are for him who uses them to do his work with.
I-II, q. 2, a. 5.

INTELLECT

Intellect and reason is the principal part of man's nature, and the specific mark of man among animals.
I-II, q. 31, a. 7.

The intellect or the intellectual soul is the life of the body.
I, q. 76, a. 1.

The human intellect is created in the image of God.
I, q. 93, a. 1.

The intellectual principle positively is incorporeal.
I, q. 75, a. 2.

The intellect can understand that it understands.
I, q. 16, a. 4, §2.

The purpose of the intellect is to understand.
I, q. 79, a. 10.

The intellect understands by division and composition.
I, q. 85, a. 5.

The intellect can abstract the general from the particular.
I, q. 44, a. 3, §3.

The intellect is always right about first principles.
I, q. 17, a. 3, §2.

The intellect conceives many things (spiritual values) unknown to the senses.
I, q. 78, a. 4, §4.

The speculative intellect is directed solely to understanding, the practical intellect solely to action.
I, q. 79, a. 11.

The practical intellect intends the fulfilment of spiritual values; the goal of the speculative intellect is the comprehension of truth.
I, q. 14, a. 16.

The corporeal sense of sight cannot be elevated to the spiritual values; but the spiritual intellect can be lifted up to them. Similarly, the intellect is able to conceive general or abstract concepts, while the sight can only see concrete things.
I, q. 12, a. 4, §3.

It is possible to the intellect to understand God (divine value).
1, q. 12, a. 4.

The intellect cannot be guided by the senses to the comprehension of the spiritual essence of God.
I, q. 12, a. 12.

The stronger intellect, having a deeper understanding of a principle, can itself draw the conclusions, which must be explained separately to the weaker intellect.
I, q. 12, a. 8.

The intellect attains to perfection so far as it knows the essence of what is before it.
I-II, q. 3, a. 8.

Existence also is in the intellect.
I, q. 16, a. 3, §1.

INTELLECT, PRACTICAL
The practical intellect uses truth (and falsity) to action.
I, q. 79, a. 11, §2.

INTELLECTUAL
The intellectual nature immediately apprehends the truth, whereunto the rational nature arrives by the inquiry of reason; and therefore what intellect apprehends, reason attains by a process of making its way thither.
I-II, q. 5, a. 1, §1.

There must be some incorporeal value ideas . . . The perfection of the moral world is accomplished in intellectual value ideas.
I, q. 50, a. 1.

Things are intellectual from the very fact that they are immaterial.
I. q. 79, a. 3. (Ed. note: An expressive diction uses the positive word **intellectual** instead of the negative term **immaterial**. Only the materialists are always aware of the immateriality of the intellectual, pronouncing it also on irrelevant occasions.)

INTELLIGENCE
The prime author of the spiritual universe is intelligence.
C.G. I, 1, §1.

The intelligence is the same power as the intellect.
I, q. 79, a. 10.

INTEMPERANCE
Intemperance turns rather upon certain adventitious delights and desires than upon desires and delights that are natural.
II.II, q. 142, a. 3.

INTENTION

Mere intentions cannot produce natural changes.
I, q. 67, a. 3.

That which is first in the order of intention is a sort of principle moving the desire.
I-II, q. 1, a. 4.

Intention regards the end as the terminus of the motion of the will.
I-II, q. 12, a. 2.

What is beside the intention of the speaker is accidental.
II-II, q. 110, a. 1.

INTERCOURSE

The use of sexual intercourse is directed to the preservation of the whole race of mankind.
II-II, q. 153, a. 2.

Man in sexual intercourse is an animal.
I, q. 98, a. 2, §3.

There is an active and a passive principle in every sexual intercourse.
I, q. 98, a. 2.

INTEREST

The difference of interests and pursuits in life between man and man is due to the diversity of things in which the character of the final good is sought.
I-II, q. 1, a. 7, §2.

INTERPRETATION

In judging persons, we ought to lean in our interpretation to the better side.
II-II, q. 60, a. 4, §3.

Interpretation has place in doubtful cases.
II-II, q. 120, a. 1, §3.

INTOXICATION

Heat and high spirits, and disregard of dangers and deficiencies, are found in men under the excitement of drink.
I-II, q. 50, a. 6.

INTUITION

By the aid of intuition principles are apprehended, such principles as are naturally knowable, both in speculative and in practical matters.
I-II, q. 58, a. 4.

The habit that perfects the intellect for the consideration of something known of itself is called intuition.

I-II, q. 57, a. 2.

IRASCIBILITY

The irascible faculty in man is naturally subject to reason; and therefore its act is natural to man so far as it is according to reason; and so far as it is beside the order of reason it is against the nature of man.

II-II, q. 158, a. 2, §4.

Good and evil, inasmuch as it bears a character of arduousness or difficulty, is the object of the irascible faculty.

I-II, q. 23, a. 1.

J

JEST

Things done in jest in their kind are not directed to any end, but the pleasure that comes of doing them is directed to the recreation and rest of the mind.
II-II, q. 168, a. 2, §3.

Jests ought to suit the matter in hand and the person speaking.
II-II, q. 168, a. 2, §1.

Actions done in jest are not referred to any external end, but are simply directed to the good of the author of the jest, his delight or recreation.
I-II, q. 1, a. 6, §1.

JOY

There is in the intellectual appetite, or will, a pleasure which is called joy, but not a bodily pleasure.
I-II, q. 31, a. 4.

JUDGE

No one is judge in his own case.
II-II, q. 64, a. 5, §2.

The judge has care of the common good, which is justice.
I-II, q. 19, a. 10.

The judge does not pass a judicial sentence of his own, but by public authority.
II-II, q. 67, a. 4.

No one can sit as judge except over one who is in some way his subject, whether by delegation or by ordinary authority.
II-II, q. 67, a. 1.

JUDGMENT

Judgment concerns wisdom.
I, q. 1, a. 6, §3.

It is easier to find a few wise men capable of framing right laws, than to find the many who would be requisite to judge rightly of particular cases.
I-II, q. 95, a. 1, §2.

Every man judges according as he knows.
II-II, q. 77, a. 3, §1.

We judge a thing by its essentials.
I, q. 16, a. 1.

A perfect judgment can be formed only by including all relevant things.
I, q. 84, a. 8.

Every one ought to judge of things as they are.
II-II, q. 60, a. 4, §2.

With the pain of loss one is afflicted even in human judgment without fault, but not without reason.
II-II, q. 108, a. 4, §2.

Even according to the just judgment a man should be executed, inasmuch as he is a murderer, but live, inasmuch as he is a human being.
I, q. 19, a. 6.

To God alone belongs judgment of life and death.
II-II, q. 64, a. 5.

The judgment of man cannot pass upon interior acts, which are hidden, but only about exterior movements which appear: and yet for the perfection of virtue rectitude in both sorts of acts is necessary.
I-II, q. 91, a. 4.

In a judgment we should rather make a point of judging a man to be good, unless manifest reason appear to the contrary.
II-II, q. 60, a. 4, §2.

In judging of things, there is no question of any good or evil to accrue to the thing that we judge of: for the thing is not hurt, however we judge of it.
II-II, q. 60, a. 4, §2.

Because fear is born of love, the same judgment seems to hold of love and of fear.
II-II, q. 126, a. 1.

JURISDICTION

No one justly punishes another, unless he be subject to his jurisdiction.
II-II, q. 65, a. 2.

JUST

One acts justly when one acts according to the law.
I. q. 21, a. 1, §2.

JUSTICE

Divine justice is properly called truth.
I, q. 21, a. 2. Vide Introduction.

Justice is not directed to the guidance of any cognitive act; for we are not called just for the fact of our knowing anything correctly.
II-II, q. 58, a. 4.

The consideration of justice belongs to reason only.
II-II, q. 159, a. 2.

The proper office of justice in its place among virtues is to direct a man in his dealings with another. For justice involves a certain equality; for the things that are equalized are said to be adjusted; and equality is a relation of one thing with another.
II-II, q. 57, a. 1.

It belongs to justice to rectify human acts.
II-II, q. 58, a. 2.

Justice is a certain rectitude of mind whereby a man does what he ought to do in any matter.
I-II, q. 61, a. 4.

Justice not only makes a man prompt of will for just deeds, but also makes him act justly.
I-II, q. 56, a. 3.

It belongs to justice to establish equality in the dealings of one man with another.
II-II, q. 79, a. 1.

Justice deals with acts that are about exterior things. But moral virtues are concerned with interior passions.
I-II, q. 64, a. 2.

The subject-matter of justice is exterior conduct.
II-II, q. 58, a. 11.

Distributive justice presides over distributions, while commutative justice presides over the exchanges that may have place between two individuals.
II-II, q. 61, a. 3.

Justice is conversant with the exterior acts of distribution and exchange.
II-II, q. 61, a. 3.

Justice is a habit, whereby with a standing and abiding will one gives every one his due.
II-II, q. 58, a. 1.

JUSTICE, LEGAL

Any virtue, inasmuch as it is directed to the good of the commonwealth, may be called legal justice.
II-II, q. 58, a. 6.

K

KEEPING ONE'S WORD
To keep one's word is an obligation of natural law, and nothing can be commanded a man against an obligation of natural law.
II-II, q. 70, a. 1, §2.

KILLING
Human law cannot allow as lawful the killing of a man unduly. But there is nothing undue in the killing of malefactors or enemies of the commonwealth.
I-II, q. 100, a. 8, §3.

Though to kill a man, while he abides in his native dignity, be a thing of itself evil, yet to kill a man who is a sinner may be good.
II-II, q. 64, a. 2, §3.

KINDNESS
To everyone kindness is to be known by preference in the matter wherein he is connected with us. Such is the general rule, but it admits of variation for variety of places and times and businesses.
II-II, q. 31, a. 3.

The return of kindness always strives to the best of the person's ability to give back something greater than has been received.
II-II, q. 106, a. 6.

If after repeated kindness the other increases his ingratitude and becomes worse, the benefactor ought to desist from bestowing kindness.
II-II, q. 107, a. 4.

He who bestows a kindness ought not to pose as a punisher of

ingratitude, but rather as a benevolent physician, seeking to cure ingratitude by reiterated acts of kindness.
II-II, q. 107, a. 4, §3.

He who bestows a kindness on an ungrateful person, does not give an occasion of sin, but rather of gratitude and love. If the recipient thence takes occasion of ingratitude, that is not to be imputed to the giver.
II-II, q. 107, a. 4, §2.

The return of kindness has regard to the benefit, as the benefit was in the will of the benefactor.
II-II, q. 106, a. 6.

KING

A king is, by virtue of his power, present in the whole kingdom, although not in every place.
I, q. 8, a. 3.

KINSMEN

Friendship between kinsmen is more stable.
II-II, q. 26, a. 8.

KISSING

Kissing, embracing, or touching, are not acts that of their own imply mortal sin: for they may be done without passion, either in compliance with the custom of the country, or for some necessity or reasonable cause.
II-II, q. 154, a. 4.

Though kisses and touches do not of themselves hinder the good of human offspring, yet they proceed from lust, which is the root of such hindrance.
II-II, q. 154, a. 4, §2.

KNOWABLE

A thing is knowable as far as it exists.
I, q. 16, a. 3.

KNOWLEDGE

In man it is specially ordered to minister to intellectual knowledge.
II-II, q. 167, a. 2.

On the side of the soul man is inclined to desire knowledge. On the other hand, man is inclined on the side of his bodily nature to shun the labor of searching after knowledge.
II-II, q. 166, a. 2, §3.

Knowledge is different from wisdom.
I, q. 25, a. 5, 1.

Knowledge of truth is in itself good.
II-II, q. 167, a. 1. Vide Introduction.

The faculty of knowledge does not know anything actually without some attention and advertence.
C. G. I, 55, §2.

Human knowledge is derived from sensible objects.
II-II, q. 85, a. 1.

The intellectual knowledge is both more perfect and better known, inasmuch as intellect reflects on its own act more than sense. Intellectual knowledge is also more loved; for there is none that would not rather forego his bodily sight than his mental vision.
I-II, q. 31, a. 5.

Knowledge refers to material nature and to spiritual God.
I, q. 64, a. 1.

Corporeal matters cannot influence spiritual matters.
I, q. 84, a. 6.

Things of sense are more known to us than things of intellect.
I-II, q. 31, a. 5.

Our knowledge of the divine creator is derived from our knowledge of His created things.
I, q. 39, a. 1.

Human knowledge advances from a thing known to another.
I, q. 58, a. 3.

When a man knows an effect, and knows that it has a cause, there is in him an outstanding natural desire of knowing the essence of the cause.
I-II, q. 3, a. 8.

Man knows future events only through their causes.
I, q. 57, a. 3, §1.

Human knowledge is caused by the things known. It is further to be considered that human knowledge is liable to many deceptions, especially as to points of detail in such a matter as human acts.
I-II, q. q, a. 3.

The knowledge that comes by the senses, in man as well as in other animals, is ordered to the end of maintenance of the body; because by means of this knowledge men and other animals avoid what is hurtful, and seek out what is necessary for their sustenance.
II-II, q. 167, a. 2.

When good is known, the opposite evil is known.
C.G. I, 71, §1.

When the teacher communicates knowledge to his disciple, it can, strictly speaking, not be said that knowledge itself begets knowledge.

I, q. 76, a. 2, §5.

Knowledge is an occasion to man of trusting in himself, and therefore of neglecting to give himself over entirely to God.
II-II, q. 82, a. 3, §3.

KNOWLEDGE, LEGAL

Legal knowledge is a spiritual gift.
II-II, q. 71, a. 4, §2.

L

LABOR

Man cannot labor continually, because his strength is limited.
II-II, q. 158, a. 2.

Outward labor works to the increase of our accidental reward.
II-II, q. 182, a. 2, §1.

LAUGHING

Man has the faculty of laughing.
I, q. 44, a. 1, §1.

The faculty of laughing characterizes man.
I, q. 3, a. 4.

LAW

Every man is a law to himself, inasmuch as he participates in
the direction given by one who regulates him.
I-II, q. 90, a. 3, §1.

In some cases it is evil to abide by the law as it stands, and good
to overlook the words of the law, and follow the course that is
dictated by regard to justice and public expediency.
II-II, q. 120, a. 1.

Every law framed by man bears the character of a law exactly to
that extent to which it is derived from the law of nature.
I-II, q. 95, a. 2.

LAW, ETERNAL

The eternal law is the system of divine government.
I-II, q. 93, a. 4.

LAW, HUMAN

The human legal law does not punish the mere wish to murder.
I-II, q. 100, a. 9.

Human law never ought to be changed, unless the gain to the public advantage on the other side be enough to balance the loss on this head. Laws gather greatest weight by custom, and therefore they ought not lightly to be changed.
I-II, q. 97, a. 2.

LAW, KNOWLEDGE OF

All men do know the law to a certain extent, at least to the extent of the common principles of the natural law. For the rest, some men partake more and some less, in the knowledge of law.
I-II, q. 93, a. 2.

LAW, LEGAL

A private person cannot induce another to virtue efficaciously: for he can only admonish; but if his admonition is not received, he has no coercive power, which the law must have, if it is to induce people to virtue efficaciously.
I-II, q. 90, a. 3, §2.

One is said to be subject to a law as the coerced to the coercer: and in this way, virtuous and just men are not subject to the law, but only bad men.
I-II, q. 96, a. 5.

Because of wanton and saucy spirits, prone to vice, who cannot easily be moved by words, it was found necessary to provide means of restraining young people from evil by force and fear. This discipline, coercive by fear of punishment, is the discipline of the laws.
I-II, q. 95, a. 1.

If a case arises in which the observance of a law would be hurtful to the public welfare, it is not to be observed.
I-II, q. 96, a. 6.

LAW, NATURAL

The natural or essential law may be blotted out of the hearts of men by evil persuasions, or by vicious customs and corrupt habits, as among some men the note of sin was not attached to robbery, or even to unnatural vice.
I-II, q. 94, a. 4.

LAW, NORMATIVE

Law must especially regard the order that is to be followed in the attainment of happiness.
I-II, q. 90, a. 2.

The law comes to us from some higher authority.
I, q. 21, a. 1, §2.

A normative law is a rule and measure of acts, whereby one is induced to act or is restrained from action. Now the judging rule and measure of human acts is reason, it being the part of reason to direct to the goal which is the first principle of conduct. Hence a law must be some function of reason.
I-II, q. 90, a. 1.

The name of law denotes something bearing upon the general good.
I-II, q. 90, a. 2.

A law is made in view of what is in the majority of cases good.
II-II, q. 88, a. 10.

The framing of a law either belongs to the whole people, or belongs to a public personage who has care of the whole people.
I-II, q. 90, a. 3.

For a law to have the binding force which is proper to a law, it must be applied to the men who are to be regulated by it.
I-II, 90, a. 4.

Man can make a law only upon matters of which he can be a judge.
I-II, q. 91, a. 4.

Man cannot impose a law upon irrational things, however much they be subject to him: but on rational beings subject to him he can impose a law, inasmuch as by his precept or proclamation he impresses on their minds a rule, which is a principle of action.
I-II, q. 93, a. 5.

LAW, POSITIVE
The will of men by common agreement can make a thing just in matters that of themselves are not irreconcilable with natural or essential justice; and in these matters positive law has place.
II-II, q. 57, a. 2, §2.

LAW, PRECEPT OF
Precepts of law are our guide.
II-II, q. 44, a. 2.

As the negative precepts of the law forbid acts of sin, so the affirmative precepts induce to acts of virtue.
II-II, q. 33, a. 2.

Since the precepts of law are ordained to the common good, these precepts must be different according to the different kinds of communities that they are given to.
I-II, q. 100, a. 2.

Precepts in law are like the propositions in speculative sciences, where the conclusions are virtually contained in the first principles.
II-II, q. 44, a. 2.

LAW, TYRANNICAL
A tyrannical law, not being according to reason, is not a law, but rather a perversion of law; and yet inasmuch as it has something of a law about it, it intends that the citizens should be good: its aim being to make them obedient, or good for the purposes of such a government.
I-II, q. 92, a. 2, §4.

LAWGIVER
The framers of laws consider long beforehand what is to be enacted: but judgments are framed on particular facts from cases that have arisen of a sudden.
I-II, q. 95, a. 1, §2.

Lawgivers judge in the general and with an eye to futurity: but men sitting in judgment judge of the present, which they regard with love and passion; and thus their judgment is warped.
I-II, q. 95, a. 1.

LAWSUIT
In criminal cases a judge cannot pass sentence on any one unless he has an accuser.
II-II, q. 67, a. 3.

LAWYER
If a lawyer knowingly defends an unjust cause, without doubt he sins grievously.
II-II, q. 71, a. 3.

LAZINESS
Laziness is a fear of work itself as being toilsome, laziness hinders work, withdrawing the will from it.
I-II, q. 44, a. 4, §3.

LEARNING
One does not learn what one already knows.
I, q. 57, a. 5.

LEGISLATOR
Man, the human legislator, can judge only of overt acts.
I-II, q. 100, a. 9.

Legislators have their eyes on what commonly occurs, and frame their law for that: yet in some cases the observance of that law

is against the equality of justice and against the public good.
II-II, q. 120, a. 1.

Since the legislator cannot have all the individual cases in his view, he puts forward a law on the basis of the circumstances that generally occur, his aim being the public utility.
I-II, q. 96, a. 6.

LENDING

Whoever lends money, transfers the dominion of the money to the borrower. The latter therefore holds it at his own risk, and is bound to restore the sum in its entirety: wherefore the lender ought not to exact any more.
II-II, q. 78, a. 2, §5.

LIABILITY

Sin incurs liability to punishment by this, that it is the subversion of some normative order.
I-II, q. 87, a. 3.

It is plain that on the cessation of the act of sin liability to punishment remains. For an act of sin makes a man liable as a transgressor of the order of justice.
I-II, q. 87, a. 6.

LIBERALITY

Justice renders to another what is his, but liberality gives him what is the giver's own.
II-II, q. 117, a. 5.

It belongs to liberality, not to be held back by immoderate love of money either from suitable expenses or from suitable gifts. Hence liberality is conversant with gifts and expenses.
II-II, q. 117, a. 3, §3.

There is a manner of giving appertaining to liberality, whereby that is given gratuitously to another which is not due to him.
II-II, q. 63, a. 1, §1.

If the transference of a thing is absolute without its being due, as in a gift, that is not an act of justice, but of liberality.
II-II, q. 61, a. 3.

It belongs to liberality particularly, not to be held back by any inordinate affection for money from any right use of money: one upon himself—a matter of personal expenses; another upon others—a matter of gifts.
II-II, q. 117, a. 3, §3.

LIBERTINE

The libertine would wish to enjoy his pleasure without offence

of God: but with the alternatives before him he chooses to incur the displeasure of God by sinning rather than go without his gratification.
I-II, q. 78, a. 1, §2.

LIBERTY

There may be spiritual liberty or slavery either in respect of what goes on internally or of what goes on externally.
II-II, q. 184, a. 4.

As inability to sin does not diminish liberty, so neither is liberty diminished by the necessity of a will fixed on good.
II-II, q. 88, a. 4, §1.

LIE

Very many fall into lying.
II-II, q. 89, a. 1.

A lie has the character of sinfulness, not only from the damage done to a neighbor, but also from its own inordinateness.
II-II, q. 110, a. 3, §1.

He who promises anything, if he has the intention of doing what he promises, does not lie; because he does not speak contrary to what he bears in mind.
II-II, q. 110, a. 3, §5.

A jocose lie has a character of deceit from the very kind of the act, though in the intention of the speaker it be not spoken to deceive, and from the manner of speaking actually do not deceive.
II-II, q. 100, a. 3, §6.

The essential character of lying is derived from formal falsehood, or from the fact of one having the will to assert what is false: a lie is speech against one's mind.
II-II, q. 110, a. 1.

It makes no difference whether one lies in word or in action.
II-II, q. 111, a. 1.

He would not be guiltless of lying, who by nods and becks should endeavor to give any false intimation.
II-II, q. 110, a. 1, §2.

It is clear that lying is directly and formally opposed to the virtue of truthfulness.
II-II, q. 109, a. 1.

LIFE

Intelligent beings have a more perfect degree of life.
I, q. 18, a. 3.

There is a twofold life of man: one exterior, lived in our sensible and bodily nature; and in this we have no communion or converse with God. Another life is spiritual, lived in the mind.
II-II, q. 23, a. 1, §1.

To live well is to work well, or display a good activity.
I-II, q. 57, a. 5.

The same acts are not proper to man at all seasons of his life.
I, q. 99, a. 1.

Life is preserved by the movement of the heart.
I, q. 18, a. 1, §1.

Life consists in knowledge and movement.
I, q. 75, a. 1.

Life, not movement, is divine essence.
I, q. 18, a. 4.

One can realize on things alive, to what life belongs. Life obviously belongs to animals.
I, q. 18, a. 1.

An animal possesses life as long as it moves of itself.
I, q. 18, a. 1.

The work in the delight of which the whole life of a man is ordered, is called his life.
I, q. 18, a. 2, §2.

In the active life, which is busied with many things, there is less of the essence of happiness than in the contemplative life, which is busy with the one occupation of the contemplation of truth. Though at times the contemplative man is not actually engaged in contemplation, still, because he has it ready at hand, he is always able to engage in it; moreover, the very cessation for purposes of sleep or other natural occupation is ordered in his mind towards the aforesaid act of contemplation, and therefore that act seems in a manner continual.
I-II, q. 3, a. 2, §4.

Life has two meanings. One way it means the very being of the living; in another way life is taken to mean the activity on the part of the living thing by which activity the principle of life is reduced to act. Thus we speak of an active or contemplative life, or of a life of pleasure.
I-II, q. 3, a. 2, §1.

Life is a gift divinely bestowed on man.
II-II, q. 64, a. 5.

LIFE, SPIRITUAL

The principle of spiritual life is reference to ultimate value.
I-II, q. 88, a. 1.

LIGHT

The light diffuses equally in all directions, like in a circle.
I, q. 67, a. 2.

The diffusion of light occurs instantaneously.
I, q. 67, a. 2.

Light is effective: the rays of the sun warm up bodies.
I, q. 67, a. 3.

LIGHT, INTELLECTUAL

The intellect of the creature is also called the intellectual light.
I, q. 12, a. 2.

LIKENESS

Likeness derives from agreement or communication in form.
I, q. 4, a. 3.

LIMPING

Limping stems, not from the motion, but from the imperfect curvature of the leg.
I, q. 49, a. 2, §2.

LINE

Euclid's definition of the line contains the concept of the point, because he considers a line of definite length.
I, q. 85, a. 8, §2.

LIQUOR

Intoxicating liquor hinders reason in a special manner, and therefore requires a special virtue.
II-II, q. 149, a. 2, §1.

LOAN

If one grants the use of a thing, reserving a claim to the recovery of it, it is called loan or lending in things that do not fructify.
II-II, q. 61, a. 3.

LOGIC

Logical arguments cannot validate or invalidate nonlogical articles of faith.
I, q. 1, a. 8, §1.

LOSS

Loss means someone having less than he ought to have.
II-II, q. 62, a. 4.

LOT

If the point to be determined by lot is, what is to be assigned and to whom, be it a matter of property or of dignity, or of punishment, or of employment; that is called a dividing lot. If the inquiry is, what is to be done, it is called a consulting lot. If the inquiry is, what is to happen in the future, that is called a divining lot.
II-II, q. 95, a. 8.

LOVE

Loving is willing well to anyone.
I, q. 59, a. 4, §2.

One should love his fellow citizens for the sake of political virtue, whereas one loves his blood relations with natural love.
I, q. 60, a. 4.

The greater the love, the more need for it to be firm and lasting.
C. G. III, 123, §5.

A man is said to love himself, when he loves his spiritual nature.
II-II, q. 26, a. 4.

Better is it to be loved than to be respected.
II-II, q. 74, a. 2.

When one loves his neighbor for his own profit or enjoyment, he does not truly love his neighbor, but himself.
II-II, q. 44, a. 7.

A way in which we have more love of charity for those with whom we are more intimate, is that we have more varieties of love for them.
II-II, q. 26, a. 7.

In the love of desire the lover, properly speaking, loves himself, wishing for himself the good that he desires.
I-II, q. 27, a. 3.

A man ought to love himself, after God, more than any other person. For God is loved as the principle of goodness, on which the love of charity is founded; man loves himself in charity inasmuch as he is partaker in the goodness aforesaid: while his neighbor is loved on the score of partnership in that good.
II-II, q. 26, a. 4.

In the love of desire, he who desires intensely, is moved against all that stands in the way of his gaining or quietly enjoying the object of his love.
I-II, q. 28, a. 4.

Intellectual love is different from natural love.
I, q. 60, a. 1, §1. (Ed. note: The difference lies, not in the love, but in the object.)

Nothing is loved but what is known.
I-II, q. 3, a. 4, §4.

Love follows knowledge.
I, q. 60, a. 2.

Love ranks above knowledge in moving, but knowledge goes before love in attaining.
I-II, q. 3, a. 4, §4.

The intensity of love is in proportion to the nearness of the person loved to the person loving. And therefore love is to be measured out to different persons differently according to different ties that bring them near.
II-II, q. 26, a. 8.

Love even in the intellectual appetite differs from sympathy: for it involves a union of affection between the person loving and the person loved, the former counting the latter as in a manner united to himself, or belonging to himself, and being affected towards him accordingly.
II-II, q. 27, a. 2.

The first impression made on appetite by its object is called love, which is nothing else than a complacency taken in an object of appetite; and from this complacency follows movement towards the said object, which movement is desire; and finally comes rest, which is joy. So then, manifestly love is a passion.
I-II, q. 26, a. 2.

A man proves himself to love a thing the more, the more lovable the thing that he despises for its sake, and the more hateful the thing that he chooses to suffer rather than lose it.
II-II, q. 124, a. 3.

The love of a proper good is apt to perfect and better the lover: while the love of a good that is not proper to the lover is apt to waste away the lover and alter him for the worse.
I-II, q. 28, a. 5.

LOVE, NATURAL
Natural love denotes natural union.
I, q. 60, a. 5.

All natural love is well regulated, having been implanted in nature.
I, q. 60, a. 1, §3.

LOVE AND HATE

A man loves more his own good than he hates another's evil.
I-II, q. 32, a. 6, §3.

LOVER

A lover works for the good of the beloved as he works for his own.
I, q. 20, a. 2, §1.

LUST

In the commission of lust there is sexual pleasure.
I-II, q. 72, a. 2.

The lustful man wants the pleasure, to which the sin is attached, though he does not absolutely wish for the sin; for he would like to enjoy the pleasure without the sin.
II-II, q. 46, a. 2, §2.

The lust of the will, which increases the sin, is greater in the intemperate than in the incontinent.
II-II, q. 156, a. 3, §3.

LUXURY

The vice of luxury strongly moves the inferior or concupiscible appetite to its object, that is, to pleasure, and consequently throws the higher power, the reason and will, into very great disorder.
II-II, q. 153, a. 5.

It is the nature of luxury to exceed the mode and order of reason in the matter of sexual pleasures; and therefore without doubt luxury is a sin.
II-II, q. 153, a. 3.

M

MACERATION

The maceration of the body by watchings and fastings is not acceptable to God except so far as it is a work of virtue; and that it is insofar as it is done with due discretion, so that concupiscence may be restrained at the same time that nature is not overwhelmed.
II-II, q. 88, a. 2, §3.

MAGNANIMITY

Magnanimity seems to be the same as self-confidence.
II-II, q. 128, a. 1.

Because the magnanimous man does not account as great the exterior goods of fortune, he is not much elated at their presence, nor greatly dejected at their loss.
II-II, q. 129, a. 8, §3.

Magnanimity and humility are not contrary, because they proceed on different considerations.
II-II, q. 129, a. 3, §4.

Magnanimity from its name implies a reaching out of the soul to great things. A man is called magnanimous, principally from this, that he has a mind bent upon some great act.
II-II, q. 129, a. 1.

Magnanimity holds the golden mean in a presumptuous hope.
II-II, q. 21, a. 1.

MAGNIFICENCE

Magnificence in the matter of liberality adds a certain magnitude, which reaches to the idea of arduousness.
II-II, q. 128, a. 1, §1.

MAKE-UP

Women's painting of themselves is a species of counterfeit that cannot be without sin. Such painting however is not always fraught with mortal sin, but only when it is done for lasciviousness or in contempt of God.

II-II, q. 169, a. 2, §2.

MALICE

The sin that is of deliberate malice is more grievous than the sin that is of passion.

I-II, q. 78, a. 4.

MAN

Man in a metaphorical sense contains all things.

I, q. 96, a. 2.

Man is a social animal.

II-II, q. 109, a. 3, §3.

Man has a natural inclination to live in society.

I-II, q. 94, a. 2.

Man surpasses all other animals in his faculty of understanding.

I, q. 76, a. 1.

Man is properly that which he is according to reason.

II-II, q. 155, a. 1, §2.

Man excels the plants, although both of them have an erect stature.

I, q. 91, a. 3, §3.

In man there is a double nature, rational and sensitive.

I-II, q. 71, a. 2, §3.

What is man? Answer: a mortal rational animal.

I, q. 29, a. 4, §2.

Man is capable of understanding and loving God.

I, q. 93, a. 4.

Man is of the same *genus* as other animals, but he is of a different *species*.

I, q. 75, a. 3, §1.

The spiritual part of man is called the inward man, the corporeal part the outward man.

I, q. 75, a. 4, §1.

The being of man consists of soul and body, and while the being of the body depends on the soul, at the same time the being of the human soul does not depend on the body: indeed the body is for the soul.

I-II, q. 2, a. 5.

There is no difference between man and other animals in regard to the sensible world.
I, q. 78, a. 4.

Man is made in the image of God, not concerning his body, but concerning his spirit.
I, q. 3, a. 1, §2.

The majority of men possess sufficient wisdom for a reasonable way of life, but only a minority arrive at profound wisdom.
I, q. 23, a. 7, §3.

As man could not live in society without truth, so neither can he without pleasure.
II-II, q. 114, a. 2, §1.

In every man, even in the sinner, we ought to love the nature which God has made, and which is destroyed by killing.
II-II, q. 64, a. 6.

Man is more bound to take thought for his own life than for the life of his neighbor.
II-II, q. 64, a. 7.

Men could not live with one another, if they did not believe one another as declaring the truth to one another.
II-II, q. 109, a. 3, §1.

It is common to all men to love that which each one takes himself to be.
II-II, q. 25, a. 7.

Not all men take themselves to be that which they really are.
II-II, q. 25, a. 7.

All men are prone to undue pleasures, and especially the young.
I-II, q. 95, a. 1.

Man has a certain aptitude for virtue, but the perfection of virtue must accrue to him by discipline and training.
I-II, q. 95, a. 1.

In no man is the wisdom of the flesh so predominant as to spoil the whole good of his nature; and therefore there remains in man some inclination to comply with the enactments of the law.
I-II, q. 93, a. 6, §2.

Nature has given man the beginnings of the satisfaction of his wants, in giving him reason and a pair of hands; but not complete satisfaction, as to other animals, to whom she has given in sufficiency clothing and food.
I-II, q. 95, a. 1.

The life of animals and plants is preserved, not for their own sakes, but for the sake of man.
II-II, q. 64, a. 1, §1.

Man begets man.
I. q. 3, a. 8.

MANICHEE

The Manichees maintained that incorporeal or spiritual values are subject to the divine power, but that corporeal or visible things are subject to the material or mechanical power.
I, q. 8, a. 3.

MANUFACTURING

In any art of manufacturing articles that men cannot use without sin, workmen making such things would thereby sin, as directly supplying others with an occasion to sin.
II-II, q. 169, a. 2, §4.

MARRIAGE

Marriage is ordained to the good of the body, the bodily multiplication of the human race, and belongs to the active life, because husband and wife, living in the married state, are under the necessity to think of "the things of the world."
II-II, q. 152, a. 4.

MARTYR

A martyr is so called as being a witness of the faith, that faith which proposes to us to despise the things that are seen for the spiritual values that are not seen.
II-II, q. 124, a. 4.

The martyrs had greater merit of faith, not receding from the faith for persecutions.
II-II, q. 2, a. 10, §3.

Martyrs endure personal combats for the sake of the sovereign good, which is God: therefore their fortitude is above all commended.
II-II, q. 123, a. 5, §1.

There would not be patient martyrs without persecuting tyrants.
I, q. 22, a. 2, §2.

MARTYRDOM

Martyrdom consists in the due suffering of death.
II-II, q. 124, a. 3.

Martyrdom supposes a man to bear witness to his faith, showing

120

in very deed that he despises all advantages in order to arrive at invisible values.
II-II, q. 124, a. 4.

The first and principal motive of martyrdom is charity, acting in the capacity of the virtue commanding.
II-II, q. 124, a. 2, §2.

The essence of martyrdom, full and perfect, requires the suffering of death.
II-II, q. 124, a. 4.

MASTER
Man is made his own master by free-will.
II-II, 2. 64, a. 5, §3.

A rational creature is master of his own acts.
I, q. 19, a. 12, §3.

MATERIALISM
Since the old philosophers ascribed existence only to bodies, they asserted that the soul is nothing else but a body. This materialistic view is however utterly wrong. The soul is not of material, but of spiritual essence.
I, q. 75, a. 1.

Some philosophers assumed that there are no value ideas but only bodies.
I, q. 51, a. 1, §1.

The early philosophers were not aware of the meaning of understanding and of the difference between sense and intellect. They denied anything that could not be perceived by the senses thus acknowledging only corporeal existence.
I, q. 50, a. 1.

MATHEMATICS
There is no goodness in mathematics.
I, q. 16, a. 4.

MATRIMONY
Matrimony is an office of nature.
II-II, q. 100, a. 2, §6.

MATTER
The matter is for the form.
II-II, q. 55, a. 1, §2.

MATTERS, GREAT
To attack any great matters may be accounted dangerous, because to fail in such matters is very hurtful.
II-II, q. 128, a. 1, §3.

MEANING

The meaning of a word is the object which the intellect apprehends of the thing.
I, q. 5, a. 2.

A slight difference of words alters the meaning.
II-II, q. 68, a. 2, §1.

MEAN-SPIRITED

The mean-spirited are envious, because they count everything great; and whatever good happens to any one, they reckon that they have been outdone in a great matter.
II-II, q. 36, a. 1.

MEANS

What is due for the sake of something else is the means to the end.
II-II, q. 44, a. 1.

Means to the end must be commensurate with the end, as medicine with health.
II-II, q. 118, a. 1.

MEANS AND END

The knowledge of the proportion between means and end belongs to intellect and reason.
I, q. 18, a. 3.

MEASURE

A proper measure must be adequate to the object measured.
I, q. 3, a. 5, §2.

MEDICINE

Moderation in food as to quantity and quality belongs to the art of medicine, where there is question of the health of the body.
II-II, q. 146, a. 1, §2.

Bodily pleasures are like medicines against certain annoyances.
I-II, q. 35, a. 5.

A medicine is not only remedial of past sin, but is also preservative against future sin, or promotive of some good.
II-II, q. 108, a. 4.

MEDITATION

Meditation needs must be the reason of devotion, inasmuch as by meditation it is that man gets the thought of giving himself over to the service of God.
II-II, q. 82, a. 3.

MEEKNESS

Meekness particularly makes a man master of himself.
II-II, q. 157, a. 4.

Meekness properly diminishes the passion of anger.
II-II, q. 157, a. 1.

MEMBER

The exterior members move at the command of reason.
II-II, q. 168, a. 1.

MEMORY

Memory is of the past and hope of the future.
I-II, q. 50, a. 6.

Memory belongs to animal as well as to man.
I, q. 79, a. 6.

It is difficult to remember a statement word by word on account of the multitude and variety of words. A number of persons hearing the same words would not repeat them alike even after a short interval.
II-II, q. 68, a. 2, §1.

The memory of events is impaired by time, for events of ancient date easily drop from memory.
I-II, q. 48, a. 2, §2.

MERCY

To mercy it belongs to relieve misery by the bestowal of kindness.
II-II, q. 159, a. 1, §2.

Mercy does not negate justice, but fulfils it liberally.
I, q. 21, a. 3, §2.

Divine mercy delivers the penitent sinner.
I, q. 64, a. 2, §2.

The merciful God treats men more generously than is adequate to their deserts.
I, q. 21, a. 4.

MERIT

Merit signifies a being which strives for a moral goal.
I, q. 62, a. 1.

Merit and demerit are predicated in view of retribution, which is rendered according to justice.
I-II, q. 21, a. 3.

One merits and demerits by moral judgment, and not by physical acts.
I, q. 60, a. 2.

123

Merit is determined by God, and not by nature.
I, q. 63, a. 5, §3.

MERITORIOUS
Our acts are meritorious, inasmuch as they proceed from free-will.
II-II, q. 2, a. 9.

MILITARY
Military service is directed towards the duty of fighting.
I, q. 24, a. 2.

MIND
Man surpasses all other creatures by his mind.
I, q. 93, a. 6.

The prime element in man is his rational mind: while his sentient and bodily nature is of secondary importance.
II-II, q. 25, a. 7.

It is clear that man is especially the mind of man.
I-II, q. 29, a. 4.

The human mind exists, although being incorporeal, that is, only spiritual.
I, q. 75, a. 2.

The mind or intellect, not the body, has the faculty of understanding.
I, q. 75, a. 2.

The mind can comprehend itself through its own power.
I, q. 88, a. 2, §1.

The mind cannot in this mortal life be elevated to the highest spiritual values, that is, to God.
I, q. 12, a. 11.

The less the mind is absorbed in corporeal things, the more it is capable of understanding spiritual values.
I, q. 12, a. 11.

The weakness of the human mind requires to be led as it were by the hand to the knowledge and love of things spiritual, by aid of the things of sense.
II-II, q. 82, a. 3, §2.

The mind is not applied to an object otherwise than by knowing or trying to know it.
II-II, q. 166, a. 1.

MIND, DIVINE
There are in the divine mind all proper value ideas for all men.
I, q. 15, a. 2.

124

MIND'S EYE
The mind's eye, that is, the intellect evidently can see God as well as the bodily eye can see the life of another.
I, q. 12, a. 3, §2.

MIRROR, SPIRITUAL
The things can be seen in God as in a spiritual mirror.
I. q. 12, a. 9.

MISAPPREHENSION
As things are apprehended as good, which are not really good, so things are apprehended as evil which are not really evil: hence it happens sometimes that neither hatred of evil nor love of good is good.
I-II, q. 29, a. 1, §2.

MISCHIEF
The mischief-maker intends to dissolve a friendship.
II-II, q. 74, a. 1.

MISER
The miser is useful to none, not even to himself.
II-II, q. 119, a. 3.

The miser's is no easy cure.
II-II, q. 119, a. 3.

In affection to riches the miser superabounds, loving them to excess: while the prodigal falls short, not taking due care of them.
II-II, q. 119, a. 1.

MISSION
Mission signifies being sent by another person.
I, q. 43, a. 1.

MODEL, NORMATIVE
God understands many normative models proper to many human actions, and they are many value ideas.
I, q. 15, a. 2.

There are models in the divine mind, that is, model commandments of all religious things, which are also called value ideas or exemplary norms.
I, q. 44, a. 3.

MODERATION
Moderation is requisite in every virtue.
II-II, q. 141, a. 7.

MODESTY

Modesty is concerned with the attendant circumstances of pleasure in kisses, touches, and embraces.
II-II, q. 143, a. 1.

Modesty is especially concerned with the signs of sexual affection, as looks, kisses, and touches.
II-II, q. 151, a. 4.

MOIST

Moist bodies retain with difficulty, but receive easily.
I, q. 78, a. 4.

MONEY

Seasonably to give it away is one use of money.
II-II, q. 117, a. 4, §2.

Money is no aid to nature in itself, but is an invention of human contrivance for the convenience of exchange, as a measure of things saleable.
I-II, q. 2, a. 1.

By money is understood everything that has a money price.
II-II, q. 100, a. 2.

The proper and principal use of money is the consumption or disbursal of it, according as it is expended on exchanges.
II-II, q. 78, a. 1.

"All" material "things obey money" (Ecclesiastes), so far as the multitude of fools is concerned, who know only material things, which can be acquired by money.
I-II, q. 2, a. 1, §1.

MONISM

One world comprises corporeal and spiritual creatures.
I, q. 61, a. 4. Vide Transcendentalism.

MONISM AND DUALISM

The ancient philosophers, assuming only matter, made no distinction between intellect and sense, with the exception of Plato, who differentiated between them. He inconsistently also considered matter as spirit.
I, q. 75, a. 3.

MORAL

The human act which is called moral takes its species from its object, as that object stands related to the principle of human acts, which is reason.
I-II, q. 18, a. 8.

MORALITY

Some things are so necessary that without them the decent order of morality can hardly be maintained.
II-II, q. 80, a. 1.

MOTION

The beginning of anything corporeal and its ceasing to be is brought about by motion or change.
C. G. I, 15, §1.

Any motion (cause) is preceded by motion (cause).
I, q. 46, a. 1, §5.

MOVEMENT

Movement takes its course, not from the term *wherefrom*, but from the term *whereto*.
I, q. 23, a. 1, §3.

Outward movements are signs of inward dispositions.
II-II, q. 168, a. 1, §1.

The exterior movements of man manifestly are open to the direction of reason.
II-II, q. 168, a. 1.

The paying of special attention to the arrangement of outward movements is blameworthy, if it means that the outward movements are so feigned as not to tally with the inward dispositions.
II-II, q. 168, a. 1, §4.

The term *movement* actually referring to bodies is also applied to spiritual thoughts.
I, q. 73, a. 2.

Movement is not in God.
I, q. 42, a. 1, §3.

MOVER, INCORPOREAL

An incorporeal or spiritual mover differs from a univocal agent.
I, q. 25, a. 2, §3.

MOVING PRINCIPLE

The moving principle of the intention is the last end: the moving principle of the execution is the first step in the way of means to an end.
I-II, q. 1, a. 4.

MULTITUDE

The multitude makes most account of exterior goods of fortune.
II-II, q. 129, a. 8.

Multitude is a sort of quantity.
I, q. 30, a. 3, §2.

MUNIFICENCE

Munificence aims at doing a great work.
II-II, q. 134, a. 2, §3.

MURDER

In the substance of his person, a neighbor is injured openly by murder, or by imprisonment, or by beating or by maiming.
II-II, q. 61, a. 3.

MUTILATION

To mutilate a man of a member, though it be against the particular nature of the body that suffers mutilation, is still according to natural reason in view of the common good.
II-II, q. 65, a. 1.

N

NAME

A name can be given to anything that can be understood.
I, q. 13, a. 1.

Names denoting (physical) essences are often taken from external (spiritual) properties.
I, q. 18, a. 2.

Names which signify God negatively, do not at all denote His essence.
I, q. 13, a. 2.

Some are of the opinion that names, as *good, wise,* and the like, signify God negatively, although applied to Him affirmatively.
I, q. 13, a. 2. (Ed. note: This opinion is, however, incorrect. Only names, as invisible, incorporeal, and the like, denote negative attributes of God.)

The name *good* is applied to God properly or affirmatively.
I, q. 13, a. 3, §1.

NARCISSISM

The love that is set down as a cause of sin is an inordinate self-love.
I-II, 2. 77, a. 4, §1.

NATURAL

What is natural cannot be totally lost.
II-II, q. 126, a. 1.

NATURE

In a broader sense, the term *nature* denotes essence.
I, q. 29, a. 1, §4.

Nature inclines to what is proper to each.
II-II, q. 141, a. 1, §1.

Nature has attached delight to the activities that are necessary for the life of man.
II-II, q. 142, a. 1.

What is natural cannot be changed while nature remains.
C. G. I, 7, §4.

Nature does nothing in vain.
II-II, q. 158, a. 8, §2.

In the way of generation nature proceeds from imperfect to perfect things. Hence it is that in the generation of man there is first the living thing, then the animal, and lastly the man.
II-II, q. 64, a. 1.

Nature is not wanting to man in things necessary, though it has not given him weapons and clothing as to other animals, because it has given him reason and hands whereby he can acquire these things for himself.
I-II, q. 5, a. 5, §1.

NATURE, HUMAN
We are compounded of a two-fold nature, intellectual and sensible.
II-II, q. 84, a. 2.

NAVIGATION
A captain does not intend as a last end the preservation of the ship entrusted to him, because the ship is referred to something else as its end, namely, navigation.
I-II, q. 2, a. 5.

NECESSARIES
Man needs in this life the necessaries of the body for the exercise as well of contemplative as of active virtue. But for perfect happiness, which consists in the vision of God, such goods are nowise requisite.
I-II, q. 4, a. 7.

NECESSARY
Principles are reasons of necessary conclusions.
I. q. 44, a. 1, §2.

There are two ways of taking the phrase, necessary to human life. In one way we may call that necessary, without which the thing cannot be at all, as food is necessary to an animal; in another way we call that necessary, without which the thing cannot be in a suitable condition.
II-II, q. 141, a. 6.

A thing is said to be necessary in two ways. In one way that is necessary, by which the end is better attained; in another way a thing is necessary, without which something cannot take effect.

II-II, q. 83, a. 13.

NECESSITY

It does not belong to every one at pleasure to interpret and decide what is useful and what is harmful to the state. But if the danger is sudden, and brooks not the delay of having recourse to higher powers, the mere necessity carries a dispensation with it, because necessity is not amenable to law.

I-II, q. 96, a. 6.

NECESSITY, NATURAL

Some philosophers attribute the course of nature to the mechanical necessity of matter, rather than to the purposeful divine providence.

I, q. 22, a. 2, §3.

NEED

There are many needs in the community, and one individual cannot meet them all; but they are met by the community in this way, that one meets one need and another another.

II-II, q. 152, a. 2, §1.

NEEDY

Because there are many sufferers in need, and all cannot be relieved out of the same goods, there is entrusted to the discretion of every proprietor the disbursement of his own substance, that out of it he may relieve the needy.

II-II, q. 66, a. 7.

No one has it in his power to do works of mercy to all the needy; but it is enough if he does the work of mercy to those who come in his way.

II-II, q. 71, a. 1.

NEIGHBOR

The reason of love is touched upon in the mention of our neighbor.

II-II, q. 44, a. 7.

You should not love your neighbor for the sake of any profit or enjoyment, but for the reason that you wish your neighbor's good as he wishes his own good.

II-II, q. 44, a. 7.

It is not by the passions that we are brought into immediate relation with our neighbor.
II-II, q. 58, a. 9.

NON-BEING

Non-being is relatively desirable, inasmuch as the removal of an evil, which is produced by non-being, is desirable.
I, q. 5, a. 2, §3.

NOONDAY

Noonday is the middle between the two extremes of the day, which are morning and evening.
I, q. 58, a. 6, §2.

NOTHING IS MADE FROM NOTHING

The old philosophers considered only the emanation of causes which must be generated by causes. They therefore held the opinion that nothing is made from nothing. This thesis is, however, invalid for supreme reasons (first commandments) which not being preceded by other reasons emanate from nothing.
I, q. 45, a. 2, §1. Vide Creator.

NOW

Nothing of time exists except the instant *now*.
I, q. 46, a. 3.

The *now* finishes the past and starts the future.
I q. 46, a. 1, §7.

The comprehension of the now standing still occasions the comprehension of the eternity.
I, q. 10, a. 2, §1.

NUMBER

A number is necessarily odd or even.
I, q. 19, a. 3.

God cannot make the number four greater than it is, because it would be another number, if it were greater.
I, q. 25, a. 6.

NUMERAL

Numeral terms do not signify anything real or positive in the divine being or in the spiritual value.
I, q. 30, a. 3.

O

OATH

For the greater certainty of the evidence, the witness's oath is required.
II-II, q. 70, a. 4, §3.

An oath is a lawful and virtuous thing in itself, as is evident from its origin and end.
II-II, q. 89, a. 2.

Oaths are taken to justify men and put an end to disputes. But an oath works to the evil of a man through his using it badly, without necessity and due caution.
II-II, q. 89, a. 2.

OBEDIENCE

Obedience, like any other virtue, ought to have a ready will for its own proper object, and not for anything inconsistent with that object.
II-II, q. 104, a. 2, §3.

Among the many other things that inferiors are bound to render to their superiors, this is one thing special, that they are bound to obey their commands. Hence obedience is a special virtue, and its special object is a command, tacit or express.
II-II, q. 104, a. 2.

The duty of obedience to a superior in matters to which the right of his superiority extends, is a duty binding in justice.
II-II, q. 69, a. 1.

OBJECTION

Objections against faith are not physical but spiritual arguments.
I, q. 1, a. 8.

ODOR

Odor is emitted by the body affected by heat.
I, q. 78, a. 3.

OFFENSIVE

He who takes the offensive comes on as having the upper hand.
II-II, q. 123, a. 6, §1.

OFFERING

An offering is directly so called when something is offered to God, even though nothing be done about it: as pence or loaves are said to be offered, nothing being done about them. Hence every sacrifice is an offering, but not vice versa.
II-II, q. 85, a. 3, §3.

OFFICE

An office is so called in relation to action: rank or grade, in regard of order of superiority or inferiority.
II-II, q. 183, a. 1, §3.

OFFSPRING

It is natural for the human species for the male to be anxious to know his own offspring for certain, because he has the education of that offspring; but this certainty would be destroyed if there were promiscuous intercourse.
II-II, q. 154, a. 2.

OLD AGE

The weakness of old age is equal to that of infancy.
I, q. 99, a. 1.

Old age is contrary to prodigality.
II-II, q. 119, a. 3.

OLD MAN

The reason of old men ought to be active for the instruction of others.
II-II, q. 149, a. 6.

OLIVE

An olive must come from the seed of an olive.
I, q. 25, a. 5.

OMISSION

Others say that in a sin of omission no act is requisite, for the mere failure to do what one is bound to do is sinful. The sin of omission is then only when a person leaves out an act that he is competent to do or not to do.
I-II, q. 71, a. 5.

OMNIPOTENCE

Divine omnipotence does not cancel impossibility and necessity.
I, q. 25, a. 3, §4.

God is omnipotent only in reference to things which do not involve a contradiction.
I, q. 25, a. 3.

ONE

The concept of the one implies indivisibility.
I, q. 85, a. 8.

OPINION

Some acts of the intellect involve thinking without firm assent, adhering to one side, but with dread of the other, as in opinion.
II-II, q. 1, a. 1.

OPPORTUNITY

By riches and positions of authority and friends there is given us opportunity for action.
II-II, q. 129, a. 8.

OPTIMISM

The good will always survive.
I, q. 49, a. 3.

Under existing circumstances, the world cannot be better.
I, q. 25, a. 6, §3.

Nature procures its effects most of the time.
I, q. 63, a. 9.

ORDER

Order always points to a principle.
I, q. 42, a. 1.

The due order is for appetite to be subject to the guidance of reason.
II-II, q. 125, a. 1.

Order involves some sort of priority and posteriority.
II-II, q. 26, a. 1.

ORIGINAL

We can envision the original from the likeness of its image.
I, q. 12, a. 9, §2.

OWL

The owl is dazzled by the light of the day.
I, q. 1, a. 5, §1.

OWN

That is said to be every person's own, which is due to him on the principle of proportionate equality.
II-II, q. 58, a. 11.

P

PAIN
Pain is better than fault.
l, q. 48, a. 6, §1.

Absolutely and of itself interior pain weighs heavier than exterior pain; a sign whereof is the fact of exterior pain being voluntarily entered upon to avoid that which is interior.
I-II, q. 35, a. 7.

PARDON
If the person who has suffered the injury is willing to pardon it, the sovereign, having full power in the state, can lawfully discharge the guilty party, if he sees that course to be not prejudicial to the public interest.
II-II, q. 67, a. 4.

PARENTS
No benefactor's benefaction is so great as that of parents; and therefore in the return of benefits parents' claims are to be preferred to all others, unless there be a preponderant claim of necessity on another side.
II-II, q. 31, a. 3, §3.

It belongs to natural affection to worship parents and country.
II-II, q. 101, a. 1.

According to the commandment of God, parents are to be honored in point of nature and tie of kindred: but they are to be "hated" inasmuch as they stand in the way of our approaching the perfection of divine justice.
II-II, q. 34, a. 3, §1.

PART
Every part is referred to the whole.
I-II, q. 90, a. 2.

A part is threefold—integral, as wall, roof, and foundation are parts of a house; subjective, as ox and lion are parts of animal; and potential, as nutritive and sensitive are parts of the soul.
II-II, q. 48, a. 1.

PARTICIPATION
Plato maintained that corporeal man participates or believes in the world of spiritual value ideas by assimilating to them his conduct, which derives its valuable character from them.
I, q. 65, a. 4.

PARTNERSHIP
Partnership in the full participation of happiness, which is the reason for loving our neighbor, is a greater reason for love than partnership in happiness by way of redundance and overflow, which is the reason for loving our own body.
II-II, q. 26, a. 5.

We see that disputes arise not uncommonly among those who have any possession in joint stock.
II-II, q. 66, a. 2.

PASSION
Passion quickly passes off.
II-II, q. 156, a. 3.

Interior passions are mainsprings of exterior actions, or obstacles to the same.
II-II, q. 157, a. 1.

A man under passion utters the declaration with his lips that such a thing ought not to be done, still in his inward heart he is of opinion that it is a thing to do.
I-II, q. 77, a. 2, §5.

In passion considered absolutely, there is no character of merit or demerit, praise or blame.
II-II, q. 158, a. 2, §1.

Passions in themselves are value-neutral, convertible to good or to evil, according as they are capable of according with reason or not according with it.
I-II, q. 59, a. 1.

If by vice is meant a habit whereby one does amiss, it is manifest that no passion is a vice. But if by vice is meant sin, at that rate there is nothing to prevent passion from being a vice; and, on the other hand, there is nothing to prevent its concurring to an act of virtue.
I-II, q. 59, a. 1, §2.

Only the motions of the sensitive appetite are termed passions.
II-II, q. 58. a. 9.

Passion is properly found where there is a bodily alteration; and that takes place in the act of the sensitive appetite; whereas in the act of the intellectual appetite there is not required any bodily alteration, because that appetite is not a function of any bodily organ.
I-II, q. 22, a. 3.

Blinding the judgment of reason, whence depends the goodness of the moral act, passions diminish the goodness of the act: for it is more praiseworthy to do a work of charity on the judgment of reason than on the mere passion of pity. Passion is, however, a sign of a greater moral goodness, when a man by the judgment of his reason chooses to be affected by some passion, that he may work more readily with the co-operation of the sensitive appetite; and thus passion adds to the goodness of the action.
I-II, q. 24, a. 3, §1.

There are no passions in God.
I, q. 21, a. 1.

PAST
The statement that the past should not have happened contains a contradiction.
I, q. 25, a. 4.

PATERNITY
The reason why a wife is not allowed more than one husband at a time is because otherwise paternity would be uncertain.
C. G. III, 123, §5.

PATIENCE
As patience is necessary in what is done against us, so also in what is said against us.
II-II, q. 72, a. 3.

The endurance of any evils whatever may belong to patience.
II-II, q. 136, a. 4, §1.

A man is called patient, because he behaves himself commendably in suffering present hurts without inordinate sadness.
II-II, q. 136, a. 4, §2.

PEACE
Peace belongs to the last end of man, because it stands in relation to happiness as well antecedently as consequently. Antecedently, inasmuch as all perturbing and impeding causes are

already removed from the way of the last end; consequently, inasmuch as man, when he has gained his last end, remains at peace with his desire at rest.
I-II, q. 3, a. 4, §1.

The peace of the commonwealth is in itself good, and is not rendered evil by the evil use that some make of it, for there are many others who use it well; and by it much greater evils are prevented, as homicides and sacrilege, than the evils that are occasioned by it, which evils principally belong to the class of sins of the flesh.
II-II, q. 123, a. 5, §3.

A double union is of the essence of peace.
II-II, q. 29, a. 3.

PENAL

Penal evils come to be in the present, even by the will of God.
I-II, q. 39, a. 2, §3.

PENALTY

Penalty should be meted out to the sinner.
I, q. 49, a. 1.

Even the penalty that is inflicted according to human laws is not always medicinal to him that is punished, but to others, as when a robber is hung.
I-II, q. 87, a. 3, §2.

It is to be noted that sometimes a thing wears the look of a penal infliction, and yet has not the absolute character of punishment.
I-II, q. 87, a. 7. (Ed. note: The most famous case in point: Job who is not being punished, but probed.)

PENITENCE

Penitents, to recover their soul's health, follow a sort of dietary scheme of abstinence from things delightful.
II-II, q. 142, a. 1.

The innocent is nobler than the penitent. Yet God sometimes rejoices more over the latter, who overcomes his sin humbly and fervently.
I, q. 20, a. 4, §4.

PEOPLE

People is a multitude of men belonging to an order.
I, q. 31, a. 1, §2.

PERFECT

Perfect men do fall at times into some sins by the infirmity of the

140

flesh; but they are not scandalized in the proper sense of the word scandal, by the sayings or doings of others.
II-II, q. 43, a. 5, §3.

It is the property of the perfect to do what they do according to the rule of reason.
II-II, q. 43, a. 6.

In the order of being, less perfect things exist for the sake of the more perfect.
II-II, q. 64, a. 1.

The sins of the perfect consist of the most part in sudden impulses, which being hidden cannot give scandal.
II-II, q. 43, a. 6.

PERFECTION

Everything is perfect so far as it is in act; for potentiality without actuality is imperfect.
I-II, q. 3, a. 2.

It is a point of the perfection of man that he should know himself; but that he should be known by others is no point of his perfection, and therefore not a thing to be of itself desired.
II-II, q. 132, a. 1, §3.

Man cannot achieve his highest perfection at once.
I, q. 62, a. 5   §1.

Perfection develops not only from inclination, but also through aiming at a goal.
I, q. 59, a. 3, §2.

Man has from birth a certain perfection of his nature, that which belongs to the essence of his species; and there is another perfection to which he is brought by growth.
II-II, q. 184, a. 3, §3.

Since every being seeks its own perfection, a man seeks that as his last end which he seeks as his perfect and crowning good.
I-II, q. 1, a. 5.

PERJURY

He who swears to do an unlawful act, in swearing incurs the guilt of perjury for lack of justice.
II-II, q. 98, a. 2, §1.

Perjury is manifestly a sin against religion, the virtue which has for its office to show reverence to God.
II-II, q. 98, a. 2.

PERMANENCE

Man desires permanence in the good that he has. But the goods of this life are transient, as life itself is transient, which we desire, and would wish permanently to hold.
I-II, q. 5, a. 3.

PERSEVERANCE

It belongs to perseverance to endure long continuance according as is necessary.
II-II, q. 137. a. 1.

Perseverance in the midst of sorrows is not virtue, but something less than virtue.
I-II, q. 58, a. 3, §2.

A man should not be brought to the point of desisting from his enterprise; and to this Tully assigns perseverance.
II-II, q. 128, a. 1.

PERSISTENCE

Long persistence in good, even to the complete accomplishment of the same, belongs to a special virtue.
II-II, q. 137, a. 1.

PERSON

The name *person* characterizes a man of high dignity.
I, q. 29, a. 3, §2.

The name *person* in a spiritual sense can be appropriately attached to God.
I, q. 29, a. 3.

PESSIMISM

Evil prevails in the majority of cases concerning men.
I, q. 49, a. 3, §5.

More men follow the sense than the reason.
I, q. 49, a. 3, §5.

PETTY

The pettily economical man falls short of the proportion which there ought in reason to exist between expense and work.
II-II, q. 135, a. 1.

PHILOSOPHY

We find different divisions of philosophy (natural and spiritual) according to the different classes of things (natural and spiritual).
C. G. II, 4, §1.

Though the study of philosophy in itself is lawful and praiseworthy, still some philosophers abuse it to assail the faith.
II-II, q. 167, a. 1, §3. Vide Logic.

The ancient philosophers assumed only a material principle.
I, q. 4, a. 1.

The old philosophers did not distinguish things of intellect from things of sense.
I-II, q. 34, a. 1.

The early philosophers at first acknowledged only physical being, to the generation which they assigned causes. Later on, they differentiated between spiritual values created by reasons and uncreated material phenomena generated by causes.
I, q. 44, a. 2.

Almost the entire study of philosophy is directed to the knowledge of God.
C. G. I, 4, §1.

It would be the height of madness in a 'plain man' to declare a philosopher's propositions false.
C. G. I, 3, §1.

PHYSICIANS
Physicians give bitter potions for the recovery of health.
I-II, q. 87, a. 7.

Physicians may lawfully apply remedies to men on a feast-day.
II-II, q. 40, a. 4.

PILFERING
The pilfering of very small things may be excused from mortal sin.
II-II, q. 66, a. 6, §3.

PLACE
All places are filled with sensible things.
I, q. 52, a. 3.

PLANT
Plants, too, have life.
I, q. 69, a. 2.

A plant performs only the movements of growth and decay.
I, q. 18, a. 3.

The plants tend to their good merely by natural disposition, without additional knowledge.
I, q. 59, a. 1.

Plants exist generally for the sake of animals.
II-II, q. 64, a. 1.

PLATO
Plato considered matter as not created by reasons but generated by causes. He thus assumed two kinds of conditions, namely, value ideas or spiritual reasons besides facts or material causes.
I, q. 15, a. 3, §3.

Plato assumed forms of natural things existing apart from matter.
I, q. 79, a. 3.

PLATO AND ARISTOTLE
Plato presupposes the separate existence of spiritual values. There is indeed something which is essentially existence and essentially good: God. Aristotle agrees with this opinion.
I, q. 6, a. 4.

PLATONIST
According to the Platonists, all sciences deal with value ideas.
I, q. 85, a. 2.

PLAY
Ease and play and other things that belong to rest, are pleasant, inasmuch as they take away the distress that is of labor.
I-II, q. 32, a. 1, §3.

PLAYER
The calling of strolling players, being directed to afford solace to men, is not in itself unlawful, nor are they in the state of sin, provided they practise their playing moderately, employing no unlawful words or actions therein, and not carrying their playing into the midst of occupations or seasons where it has no place.
II-II, q. 168, a. 3.

PLAYFULNESS
They who have too little disposition to sport and play, say nothing laughable themselves, and frown upon others saying such things, not admitting the moderate playfulness of others.
II-II, q. 168, a. 4.

PLEADINGS
In no case is it lawful for any one to plead what is false.
II-II, q. 69, a. 2.

PLEASANT

That must absolutely be most pleasant, with which he is best pleased who has the best taste.
I-II, q. 1, a. 7.

PLEASURE

We must say that some pleasures are good, and some are evil.
I-II, q. 34, a. 1.

There is no doubt that intellectual pleasures are much greater that those of sense.
I-II, q. 31, a. 5.

Men are prone to immoderate pleasures.
I-II, q. 34, a. 1.

Pleasures arise from union with a suitable object, when that is felt and known.
I-II, q. 31, a. 5.

For pleasure two things are requisite, the attainment of a fitting good, and the knowledge of that attainment. Both these requisites consist in a certain activity, for actual knowledge is an activity.
I-II. q. 32, a. 1.

Pleasure makes activity perfect.
I-II, q. 33, a. 4.

Bodily pleasures are sought after as medicines against bodily defects or annoyances, whence sundry griefs ensue.
I-II, q. 31, a. 5.

PLURALITY

Plurality derives from division.
I, q. 30, a. 3.

POETRY

Poetry employs metaphors for the purpose of representation.
I, q. 1, a. 9, §1.

POINT

A point has no parts.
I, q. 10, a. 1.

POISON

The poison of some animals can be harmful to man.
I, q. 72, a. 1.

POLLUTION

Nocturnal pollution is more likely to happen, when the thought

of carnal vices that occasions it has been attended with some attraction to such pleasures, because there remains thereof some vestige and inclination in the soul of the sleeper.
II-II, q. 154, a. 5.

If the superabundance of humor be from a culpable cause, as from excess in eating and drinking, then the nocturnal pollution has a guiltiness from its cause. But if the superabundance of humor be from no culpable cause, then the nocturnal pollution is culpable neither in itself nor in its cause.
II-II, q. 154, a. 5.

POOR

The things that some men have in superabundance, are claimed by natural law for the support of the poor.
II-II, q. 66, a. 7.

POSSESSION

A man ought not to hold exterior goods as exclusively his own, but as common possessions, so as readily to share them with others in their need.
II-II, q. 66, a. 2.

Worldly possessions can be appraised in terms of money.
I, q. 63, a. 2, §2.

Possession is firm and permanent.
I, q. 10, a. 1, §6.

POTENTIALITY

Potentiality has a certain likeness to actuality, for in the promise and potency the actuality is in a manner contained.
I-II, q. 27, a. 3. Vide Introduction.

POWER

A man who abuses the power given him, deserves to lose it.
II-II, q. 65, a. 3, §1.

As it is the height of good that one should use power well in the government of many, so it is the lowest depth of evil if one uses power ill.
I-II, q. 2, a. 4, §2.

Power is susceptible of good and of evil.
I-II, q. 2, a. 4, §2.

Coercive power is not lawfully wielded in society except by the hands of public authority.
II-II, q. 67, a. 1.

Power consists in the principle of influencing another.
I, q. 8, a. 3, §3.

Power refers to possible things.
I, q. 25, a. 3.

POWER, DIVINE

The divine power is nothing else but the divine wisdom.
I, q. 25, a. 5.

The essence of power is maintained in God, inasmuch as it is the reason of religious consequences.
I, q. 25, a. 1, §3.

PRACTICAL

Man has not only speculative, but also practical principles.
I, q. 79, a. 12.

PRAISE

We praise a man by word of mouth, to let him or others know that we have a good opinion of him, that thereby we may provoke him who is praised to do still better, and lead others who hear him praised to think well of him, and revere him and imitate him.
II-II, q. 91, a. 1.

To praise another is a thing that may be done well or ill, according as due circumstances are observed or neglected.
II-II, q. 114, a. 1, §1.

PRAYER

Prayer considered in itself cannot be continual, because we must be busy with other works.
II-II, q. 83, a. 14.

Vocal prayer is added as a certain overflow of strong volition and emotion redounding from the soul to the body.
II-II, q. 83, a. 12.

To pray for another is an office of charity.
II-II, q. 83, a. 8.

We do not pray to alter the divine plan, but to obtain what God has arranged to be fulfilled by prayers.
II-II, q. 83, a. 2.

There are three effects of prayer. One is common to all acts informed with charity, namely merit. The second effect of prayer is its own proper effect, which is to obtain by asking. The third effect of prayer is that which it produces there and then, namely, a certain spiritual reflection of mind.
II-II, q. 83, a. 13.

PRECAUTION

If one neglects to observe due precaution in his actions, he does not escape the charge of homicide, if the death of a man follows from his doing.
II-II, q. 64, a. 8.

PRECEPT

A thing falls under precept inasmuch as it has the character of being something due.
II-II, q. 44, a. 1.

PRECEPT, MORAL

Moral precepts have validity from the mere dictate of reason, even if they were nowhere enacted in the legal law.
I-II, q. 100, a. 11.

Moral precepts are derived from the law of nature.
I, q. 60, a. 5.

PREDESTINATION

The diligent would become negligent, if he were told of his unfailing predestination.
I, q. 23, a. 1, §4.

Those who are not predestined to be good, would despair, if it would be revealed to them.
I, q. 23, a. 1, §4.

God properly predestines men.
I, q. 23, a. 1.

PREDETERMINATION

Natural things are predetermined towards a goal.
I, q. 23, a. 1, §1.

PRESERVATION

The individual is disposed to preserve not only himself, but also his species.
I, q. 60, a. 5, §3.

There is in man an inclination to that natural good which he shares along with all substances, inasmuch as every substance seeks the preservation of its own being, according to its nature.
I-II, q. 94, a. 2.

PRESUMPTION

There is no presumption in setting about a work of virtue.
II-II, q. 130, a. 1, §3.

To take upon himself to do what transcends his powers, is the part of presumption.
II-II, q. 130, a. 1.

Presumption seems to apply a certain immoderation in hope.
II-II, q. 21, a. 1.

By presumption one exceeds the proportion of his power.
II-II, q. 133, a. 1.

Regarding the hope whereby a man confides in his own strength, presumption is found in a man striving for a good as possible to him, when it exceeds his ability.
II-II, q. 21, a. 1.

PRETENSE

Pretense is a part of meanness of spirit.
II-II, q. 129, a. 3, §5.

PRETENSION

One pretends to holiness in order to disseminate false doctrine.
II-II, q. 111, a. 4.

PRICE

If one party is much benefited by the commodity which he receives of the other, while the other, the seller, is not a loser by going without the article, no extra price must be put on.
II-II, q. 77, a. 1.

PRIDE

The proud man does not subject his intellect to God.
II-II, q. 162, a. 3, §1.

Proud men, delighting in their own excellence, scorn the excellence of truth.
II-II, q. 162, a. 3, §1.

Pride means an inordinate seeking to stand high.
II-II, q. 132, a. 4.

The inordinate craving after difficult good belongs to the pride of life, pride being an inordinate craving after excellence.
I-II q. 77, a. 5.

Pride is not the same thing as vainglory, but is the cause of vainglory. For pride seeks inordinately after excellence; but vainglory seeks the manifestation of that excellence.
II-II, q. 162, a. 8, §2.

PRIEST

A priest is appointed to be a sort of middleman and mediator between God and the people.
II-II, q. 86, a. 2.

PRINCIPLE

Self-evident principles are obvious as soon as they are understood.
I, q. 17, a. 3, §2.

Whoever perfectly knows the principles in the whole of their virtual extension, can have no need of the conclusions being severally proposed to him.
II-II, q. 44, a. 2.

PRINCIPLE, INTELLECTUAL

The intellectual principle has a particular existence.
I, q. 76, a. 1.

PRIORITY

Priority and posteriority are in relation to some principle.
II-II, q. 26, a. 1.

PRIVATE OWNERSHIP

A peaceful state of society is better ensured under private ownership.
II-II, q. 66, a. 2.

PRIVATION

Every want or privation has its species according to the opposite habit: for blindness and deafness differ according to the difference of sight and hearing.
II-II, q. 107, a. 2.

PRODIGAL

Impoverished prodigals cannot run to excess in giving.
II-II, q. 119, a. 3.

It is to be observed that prodigals generally fall into sins of dissipation and debauchery, because as they run into idle expenses on other accounts, so also they do not shrink from lavishing money on their pleasures.
II-II, q. 119, a. 1, §3.

In exterior behavior it belongs to the prodigal to exceed in giving, but to fail in keeping or acquiring: while it belongs to the miser to come short in giving, but to superabound in getting and keeping.
II-II, q. 119, a. 1.

PRODIGALITY

Even prodigality at times is born of covetousness: as when one

prodigally expends large sums with the intention of currying favor with persons of whom he may get money.
II-II, q. 119, a. 2, §1.

PRODUCTION

Production is an act passing into exterior matter, as building, cutting, and the like; but conduct is an act abiding in the agent, as seeing, willing, and so forth.
I-II, q. 57, a. 4.

PROHIBITION

Prohibitions refer only to evils.
I, q. 48, a. 2.

PROMISCUITY

Promiscuity is against the nature of man: the intercourse of the male with the female must be with a fixed and certain person, with whom the man must stay, not for a short period, but for a long time, even for a lifetime.
II-II, q. 154, a. 2.

PROMISE

It is a different thing promising to man and promising to God.
II-II, q. 88, a. 4.

PROMOTION

If one promotes a person to the degree of master on account of his sufficiency of learning, there the cause of the thing being due is regarded, not the person.
II-II, q. 63, a. 1.

PROMULGATION

Promulgation is necessary for the law to have force.
I-II, q. 90, a. 4.

PROOF

There are many probable ways of proof.
I, q. 47, a. 1, §3.

A proof of faith the arguments of which are not cogent, is being ridiculed by the unbelievers.
I, q. 32, a. 1.

PROPERTY

It is lawful for a man to have property of his own.
II-II, q. 66, a. 2.

PROPERTY, COMMON

Community of goods is set down as a point of natural law, not

as though it were a dictate of natural law that all things should be possessed in common, and that there should be no private property: but because the marking off of separate possessions is not done according to natural, law, but rather according to human convention, which belongs to positive law.
II-II, q. 66, a. 2, §1.

PROPERTY, PRIVATE

Every one is more careful to look after a thing that is his own private concern than after what is common to all or many: since every one avoids labor, and leaves to another to do the duty that belongs to a number of persons in common, as happens where there are many persons to wait on you.
II-II, q. 66, a. 2.

Private property is not against natural law, but is an institution supplementary to natural law invented by human reason.
II-II, q. 66, a. 2, §1.

PROPORTION

Proportion ought to exist between work and expense.
II-II, q. 135, a. 1.

PROPOSITION

The intellectual power, so far as it reasons about conclusions, has for active principle some self-evident proposition.
I-II, q. 51, a. 2.

A particular proposition cannot be deduced from a general proposition, except by means of a particular proposition.
I, q. 86, a. 2, §2.

In an affirmative proposition, the subject and the predicate denote the same thing.
I, q. 13, a. 12.

PROPRIETY

A thing is said to be proper as having a certain beauty according to the ordering of reason.
II-II, q. 145, a. 3.

A thing is called proper, as having a certain excellence worthy of honor on the score of spiritual beauty.
II-II, q. 145, a. 3.

PROSTITUTE

A sort of unlawful giving is giving for a service that is unlawful, though the giving itself is not unlawful, as when one gives to a prostitute her hire. Hence such a woman can keep what is given

to her: but if she had extorted anything in excess by fraud or guile, she would be bound to make restitution to the party of whom she had it.
II-II, q. 62, a. 5, §2.

PROVIDENCE
The divine providence is being denied by some philosophers, as Democritus and the Epicureans, who contend that the world was generated by chance.
I, q. 22, a. 2.

God's providence includes the necessary nature.
I, q. 22, a. 2, §3.

The divine providence assigns necessity to some, not to all, things.
I, q. 22, a. 22.

God provides universally for all things (good and bad).
I, q. 22, a. 2, §2.

PROVOCATION
If a man were to hold his peace on purpose to provoke his assailant to anger, that would be an act of vindictiveness.
II-II, q. 72, a. 3, §3.

PRUDENCE
Prudence is a right method of conduct.
I-II, q. 57, a. 4.

Prudence is a virtue especially necessary to human life.
I-II, q. 57, a. 5.

Prudence is in the superior after the manner of a mastercraft, but in the subject after the manner of a handicraft.
II-II, q. 47, a. 12.

PUBERTY
From the time that a human being comes to the years of puberty, if his condition is not that of a slave, he is his own master in what relates to his own person, as to contracting marriage.
II-II, q. 88, a. 8, §2.

PUNISHMENT
By punishment the equilibrium of justice is restored.
II-II, q. 108, a. 4.

Never is a man punished in spiritual goods without his own fault.
II-II, q. 108, a. 4.

Since sin is an inordinate act, it is manifest that whoever sins

153

acts against some order, and consequently must be put down and degraded from that order, which degradation is punishment.
I-II, q. 87, a. 1.

The punishments of the present life are rather medicinal than retributive.
II-II, q. 66, a. 6, §2.

The infliction of punishment is not desirable for its own sake: but punishments are inflicted as medicines for the prevention of sins, and therefore have the quality of justice in so far as they are checks upon sin.
II-II, q. 43, a. 7, §1.

A person is justly punished for a vicious act, but not for a vicious habit, if it does not proceed to act.
I-II, q. 71, a. 3, §4.

Satisfactory punishment is in some sort voluntary.
I-II, q. 87, a. 7.

It is of the nature of punishment to be contrary to the will, and to be distressing, and to be inflicted for some fault.
I-II, q. 46, a. 6, §2.

Sometimes the good are temporally punished with the wicked because they have not rebuked their sins.
II-II, q. 108, a. 4, §1.

In no court is it required that the punishment should be adapted to the fault in point of duration. For though adultery or murder is committed in a moment, it is not on that account punished with the penalty of a moment, but sometimes with perpetual imprisonment or exile, sometimes also with death.
I-II, q. 78, a. 3, §1.

God, according to the order of His wisdom, sometimes punishes sinners on the spot for the deliverance of the good; sometimes again He leaves them time to repent.
II-II, q. 64, a. 2, §2.

Punishment cannot come from God, the just Judge, except for some fault.
I-II, q. 5, a. 4.

PUNISHMENT, CAPITAL
The punishment of death is not inflicted for every mortal sin, but only for those that do irreparable mischief, or are marked by circumstances of horrible atrocity.
II-II, q. 66, a. 6, §2.

PURITY

Purity is necessary for the mind to be applied to (spiritual) God, because the human mind is sullied by being bent upon inferior (physical) things.

II-II, q. 81, a. 8.

PUSILLANIMITY

The pusillanimous man falls short of the proportion of his power, and refuses to bend his efforts to what is quite within the measure of his ability.

II-II, q. 133, a. 1.

Even pusillanimity may rise in some way from pride, in this that a man rests too much on his own judgment in pronouncing himself incompetent for things for which he is competent.

II-II, q. 133, a. 1, §3.

Q

QUALITY

Quality is a disposition of substance.

Qualities have their foundation in quantity as color in a surface.
I, q. 115, a. 3.

Opposite qualities may be found in the same subject in different respects.
II-II, q. 119, a. 1, §1.

QUANTITY

Quantity is said to be a measure of substance.
I, Q. 28, a. 2.

Every quantity consists in a certain multiplication of parts.
C. G. I.69.

A small quantity counts as nothing.
II-II, q. 66, a. 6, §3.

R

RANK, MORAL
There is nothing to hinder a thing absolutely ranking above another thing, while in a certain respect it falls short of it.
I-II, q. 71, a. 3, §1.

RAPE
It is not lawful for a women to kill herself to have her honor: because she ought not to commit on her own person the greater crime, which is suicide, to avoid a less crime to be committed by another: for it is no crime of a women to be ravished by force, if there is no consent of hers.
II-II, q. 64, a. 5, §3.

RAPIDITY
It is to be remarked that rapidity of gait comes from a man having many things in view, and being in a hurry to accomplish them.
II-II, q. 129, a. 3, §3.

RATIONAL
Rational order must be established in the matter of the passions with regard to their repugnance to reason.
I-II, q. 61, a. 2.

The rational nature exceeds the sensitive in points of the object of its knowledge, because sense can nowise be cognizant of the universal, whereof reason is cognizant.
I-II, q. 5, a. 1, §1.

The rational refers, not to animal, but to human nature.
I, q. 29, a. 4.

The rational is constituted of an intellectual essence.
I, q. 3, a. 5.

REALIZATION

Wherever there is potentiality, there is craving after its realization, and a delight in the gaining thereof, if the gainer be a sentient and cognitive being.
I-II, q. 27, a. 3.

REARING

We see in the case of all animals in which the care of male and female is requisite for the rearing of the offspring, that there is not among them promiscuous intercourse, but the male is limited to one or more females, as in all birds: whereas it is otherwise with animals in which the female alone is sufficient to rear what she bears.
II-II, q. 154, a. 2.

REASON

The spiritual world is governed by reason.
I, q. 103, a. 1, §1.

There is some first reason called God.
I, q. 9, a. 1.

There is reason and imagination in man.
I-II, q. 46, a. 7, §1.

Reason has the guidance of human acts.
I-II, q. 76, a. 1.

Reason imitates nature.
I, q. 60, a. 5.

The purpose of reason is to subdue, not sensual pleasure, but immoderation.
I, q. 98, a. 2, §3.

Reason's proper office is to rule and to govern; and therefore it is proper to every one to have reason and prudence, insofar as he has any part in ruling and governing.
II-II, q. 47, a. 12.

Reason dictates that some things are to be shunned, and some things sought; and of things to be shunned, that some are more to be shunned than others; and of things again to be sought, that some are more to be sought than others; and that the more any good is to be sought the more the opposite evil is to be shunned.
II-II, q. 125, a. 1.

Reason is the first principle of all human acts: all other principles obey reason, though in different degrees. Some obey

reason's every beck without any contradiction, as do the limbs of the body if they are in their normal state.
I-II, q. 58, a. 2.

Reason herself requires that the use of reason be sometimes interrupted.
I-II, q. 34, a. 1, §1.

Reason is discursive.
I-II, q. 45, a. 4.

As the soul rules the body, so also does reason rule the sensitive appetite.
I-II, q. 56, a. 4, §3.

The natural dominion over other creatures attaches to man in virtue of his reason.
II-II, q. 66, a. 1.

The practical reason judges and passes sentence on things to be done, as the speculative reason judges and passes sentence on things to be understood.
I-II, q. 74, a. 7.

REASONABLE

Every man, inasmuch as he is reasonable, has some share in governing according to the free choice of his reason.
II-II, q. 47, a. 12.

REASONING

The practical reason reasons about practical matters, as the speculative reason reasons about speculative matters.
I, q. 79, a. 12.

Reasoning proceeds from the return to evident first principles.
I, q. 79, a. 8.

Reasoning compares the conclusion with the principle.
I, q. 58, a. 4.

Reasoning means a lack of intuition.
C. G. I, 57, §8.

Reasoning may be compared with understanding as motion with rest.
I, q. 79, a. 8.

REBUKE

Rebuke and correction is the function of wise men and elders.
I-II, q. 32, a. 6, §3.

RECTIFICATION

The behavior of a man in regard of himself is sufficiently recti-

fied by the rectification of the passions, which is the work of the virtues.
II-II, q. 58, a. 2, §4.

The rectification of a man within himself involves attention to interior passions. But the relation of one man to another is by exterior actions.
II-II, q. 58, a. 8.

RECTITUDE
Rectitude of will is requisite for happiness.
I-II, q. 4, a. 4.

Rectitude of will is an attitude of due regard to the last end.
I-II, q. 4, a. 4.

REJOICING
One rejoices only in a thing that he loves.
I, q. 20, a. 1.

RELATION
Relation means a reference from one thing to another.
I, q. 28, a. 1.

RELATION, LOGICAL
The comparison of the understanding between man and animal is only a logical relation.
I, q. 28, a. 1.

RELATION, SOCIAL
We ought to love others, because they are nigh unto us. It does not matter whether he be called our neighbor, or our brother, or our friend, because by all these names the same relation is denoted.
II-II, q. 44, a. 7.

RELATIVISM
The tepid is cold in comparison with heat.
I, q. 50, a. 1, §1.

RELIGION
Religion is divine wisdom.
I, q. 1, a. 6.

To religion it belongs to show reverence to the one God.
II-II, q. 81, a. 3.

Religion it is that offers due worship to God.
II-II, q. 81, a. 5.

There is a religion by way of revealed reason besides the sciences by way of understanding.
I, q. 1, a. 1.

Religion derives its principles, not from scientific understanding, but from divine or revealed reason.
I, q. 1, a. 5, §2.

Religion included in sacred teachings differs in principle from theology which is a part of science. *Vide* Introduction.
I, q. 1, a. 1, §2.

Religion is a moral virtue.
II-II, q. 92, a. 1.

Religion is not a theological virtue, the object of which is the last end, but a moral virtue, the office whereof is to be concerned with what makes for that end.
II-II, q. 81, a. 5.

Religion involves interior acts as principal exercises, of themselves belonging to religion; and external acts as secondary, subordinate to acts which are interior.
II-II, q. 81, a. 7.

RELIGIOUS
Though all in general who worship God may be called religious, the name is specially given to such as dedicate their entire lives to the worship of God, keeping aloof from worldly business.
II-II, q. 81, a. 1.

REMEDY
The remedy that is efficacious against a greater evil is much more efficacious against a smaller evil.
II-II, q. 60, a. 4, §3.

REPENTANCE
Men repent their threats even unexecuted.
I, q. 19, a. 7, §2.

When one repents, one eradicates the past action.
I, q. 19, a. 7, §1.

It is false that God does not pardon them that repent, or does not turn sinners to repentance.
II-II, q. 21, a. 2.

REPRESENTATION
Every representation is a certain putting of things together, which is the proper act of reason.
II-II, q. 110, a. 1.

It is not inconsistent with spiritual values to be represented under sensible figures, because the purpose is not a materialistic metamorphosis but a better understanding.
I, q. 51, a. 3, §1.

REPROBATION

Reprobation permits a man to fall into sin, and assign punishment for sinning.
I, q. 23, a. 3.

God is said to reprobate some men.
I, q. 23, a. 3.

REPRODUCTION

Every agent reproduces itself.
I, q. 4, a. 3.

REPUTATION

A good name stands above riches.
II-II, q. 73, a. 3.

Among temporal things a good name counts for a thing of particular value, as the loss of it debars a man from many avenues to success.
II-II, q. 73, a. 2.

A good name is useful to the sinner, not only in his temporal, but even in his spiritual interest: because many are withdrawn from sin by fear of infamy; hence when they see themselves become infamous, they sin without check or bridle.
II-II, q. 33, a. 7.

RESPECT

If one promotes another to a master's degree, because he is rich, or because he is a relation of his, that is a respecting of the person.
II-II, q. 63, a. 1.

The respecting of persons is opposed to distributive justice. For the equality of distributive justice consists in this, that to different persons different things are assigned in proportion to their several dignities and deserts. If therefore one has regard to that attribute in a person, which makes the thing conferred due to him, that is no respecting of the person but a regard for the cause.
II-II, q. 63, a. 1.

RESPONSIBILITY

There is nothing to hinder one being punished for the sin of

another, as children for parents, and subjects for their masters, in so far as they are in a manner the chattels of the same.
I-II, q. 87, a. 8.

REST

The mind's rest is pleasure or delight.
II-II, q. 168, a. 2.

Man needs bodily rest to refresh his body, which cannot labor continually, because its strength is limited and proportioned to finite toil.
II-II, q. 168, a. 2.

Resting is reposing in the same place now as before.
I, q. 53, a. 2.

RESTITUTION

If one pulls down another man's house, he is bound to restitution to the extent of the value of the house.
II-II, q. 62, a. 4.

To restore is nothing else than to re-establish a man in the possession or ownership of that which is his; and thus in restitution the equality of justice is obtained by weighing thing against thing.
II-II, q. 62, a. 1.

RETRIBUTION

Justice allocates equal reward or punishment to equal merit or demerit.
I, q. 65, a. 2, §3.

Reward and punishment are meted out to rational men according to merit and fault.
I, q. 22, a. 2, §5.

Retribution according to justice is rendered to one for doing something to the profit or hurt of another.
I-II, q. 21, a. 3.

RETURN

A man may get an adequate return in two ways: in one way, as when one gives so much to receive exactly as much; in another way, one thing is adequate to, or commensurate with another thing by convention.
II-II, q. 57, a. 2.

REVENUES

Revenues are a sort of pay regularly given to the rulers, that they may maintain justice.
II-II, q. 62, a. 7.

REVERENCE

Reverence is due to God for His excellence, which is communicated to creatures, not so far as to set them on a level with God, but in some measure of participation.
II-II, q. 84, a. 1, §1.

We pay reverence to God, not for His sake, seeing that of Himself He is full of glory, but for our own sakes, because by reverencing God our mind is made subject to Him, and in that subjection its perfection consists.
II-II, q. 81, a. 7.

It is a dictate of natural reason that a man should perform some acts by way of reverence to God.
II-II, q. 81, a. 1.

REWARD

Honor is not the reward of virtue for which the virtuous men work, but they receive honor from men in lieu of a reward, inasmuch as men have nothing greater to give them. But the true reward of virtue is happiness itself.
I-II, q. 2, a. 2, §1.

RICHES

If the love of riches grows so far as to be preferred to charity, one hesitates not to act against the love of God and of his neighbor.
II-II, q. 118, a. 4.

They who place their end in riches have a desire of riches to infinity; but they who seek riches for the necessaries of life, desire limited wealth, sufficient for the necessaries of life.
I-II, q. 30, a. 4.

The desire of natural riches is not boundless, because a certain measure of riches is sufficient for nature: but the desire of artificial riches is boundless, not however, in the same way as the desire of the supreme good.
I-II, q. 2, a. 1, §3.

Natural riches are all those aids which go to the supply of natural wants, like meat and drink, clothing, means of transportation, habitation, and the rest. Artificial riches take the form of money.
I-II, q. 2, a. 1.

In exterior riches one man cannot have superabundance without

another being in want, since temporal goods cannot be simultaneously possessed by many.
II-II, q. 118, a. 1, §2.

RIGHT
Right action always supposes a certain disposition of the agent.
II-II, q. 57, a. 1.

ROBBERY
One is called a good robber, because he operates in a manner calculated to gain his goal.
I-II, q. 92, a. 1.

If one takes the thing of another openly, it is called robbery.
II-II, q. 61, a. 3.

Robbery involves a certain amount of violence and constraint, whereby a man's own is taken away from him contrary to justice.
II-II, q. 66, a. 8.

Robbery is a more grievous sin than theft, because violence is more directly opposed to the will than ignorance. There is also another reason: because by robbery not only is loss inflicted on another in his property, but there is also something of personal insult or injury enacted.
II-II, q. 66, a. 9.

ROBE
They who are in positions of dignity, wear more costly robes than other men, not for their own glorification, but to signify the excellence of their office.
II-II, q. 169, a. 1, §2.

ROOT
The root of the plant corresponds to the human mouth.
I, q. 91, a. 3, §3.

RULE
A rule is called despotic or royal by which a man governs over slaves or free subjects.
I, q. 81, a. 3, §2.

A rule is a principle of action.
I-II, q. 93, a. 5.

RULER
If rulers exact from their subjects what is due in justice for the maintenance of the common weal, that is not robbery, even though force be used over it.
II-II, q. 66, a. 8, §3.

To rulers public authority is entrusted to the end that they may be guardians of justice; and therefore it is not lawful for them to use force and coercion except according to the tenor of justice, either fighting against foreign enemies, or against citizens, punishing evil-doers.
II-II, q. 66, a. 8.

Rulers, who are bound to maintain justice in the land, are bound to restitution, if by their shortcoming robbers increase; because the revenues that they have are a sort of pay regularly given to this end, that they may maintain justice.
II-II, q. 62, a. 7.

RULES OF CONDUCT
Man takes from his last end the rules of conduct for his whole life.
I-II, q. 1, a. 5.

RUNNING
Running abstractly denotes to run.
I, q. 18, a. 2.

S

SACRED

A thing is called sacred from its being ordained to divine worship.
II-II, q. 99, a. 1.

SACRIFICE

The sacrifice that is offered outwardly, signifies the inward spiritual sacrifice whereby the soul offers itself to God.
II-II, q. 85, a. 2.

There is one thing that is paid to God alone, namely, sacrifice.
II-II, q. 84, a. 1, §1.

SACRILEGE

Every piece of irreverence to sacred things is something of an injury to God, and bears the character of sacrilege.
II-II, q. 99, a. 1.

SADNESS

The mind should not be crushed and broken by sadness, and fall from its greatness in face of the difficulty of imminent evils.
II-II, q. 128, a. 1.

Among other passions sadness operates powerfully in hindering the good of reason.
II-II, q. 136, a. 1.

We get sad over what we count evil or cheap.
II-II, q. 35, a. 1, §3.

A man is saddened at another's good, inasmuch as the person to whom the good comes is unworthy.
II-II, q. 36, a. 2.

SAINT

A propitious predestination can be helped by the prayers of the saints.
I, q. 23, a. 8.

SAKE, OWN

We may cling to another either for his own sake or because by him we come to something else.
II-II, q. 17, a. 6.

In every department that which is for its own sake and in its own ordinary right, takes precedence of that which is for the sake of something else.
II-II, q. 44, a. 1.

SALE

That cannot be a due matter of sale, of which the seller is not the owner.
II-II, q. 100, a. 1.

SALVATION

The final salvation of man consists in a supernatural vision of God.
II-II, q. 2, a. 3.

The whole salvation of man rests in God.
I, q. 1, a. 1.

SAME

It is impossible that the same be a proper likeness of different things.
I, q. 55, a. 3, §3.

SAVAGERY

The name of savagery, or brutality, is so called from the likeness that it bears to wild beasts, who are also called savage.
II-II, q. 159, a. 2.

SAYINGS

Saying or doings, wherein nothing is sought beyond amusement, are spoken of as things said or done in sport or jest.
II-II, q. 168, a. 2.

SCANDAL

For the avoiding of scandal or turmoil a man ought to abate something of his right.
I-II, q. 96, a. 4.

Active scandal as it occurs ordinarily, when one intends by his inordinate word or deed to draw another to sin, derives the character of a special sin from the intention of a special end.
II-II, q. 43, a. 3.

SCIENCE

Science perfects the intellect in regard of what is a final goal in this or that kind of knowable things.
I-II, q. 57, a. 2.

The dignity of a science lies in its certainty.
I, q. 1. a. 5.

One science is said to be more dignified than another because of its higher evidence or because of its more excellent subject-matter.
I, q. 1, a. 5.

Science attempts to explore the causes of the effects.
I, q. 19, a. 5.

According to Plato, spiritual science of value ideas does not stem from natural science of physical phenomena, from which even the latter does not entirely develop.
I, q. 84, a. 6.

Speculative science, being desired as some sort of good by the student of it, is comprehended under a complete and perfect good.
I-II, q. 1, a. 6, §2.

SCIENCE, APPLIED

The perfection of an applied science increases with the examination of the particular things in the field of action.
I, q. 22, a. 3, §1.

SCIENCE, SPIRITUAL

According to Plato, spiritual science does not apprehend material things (apprehended in natural science), but spiritual values.
I, q. 84, a. 1.

SCIENTIFIC

In the case of a man holding a conclusion without knowing the demonstration that leads to it, it is manifest that he has no scientific knowledge on that point, but opinion only.
II-II, q. 5, a. 3.

SECRET

Man conceals his secrets.
I, q. 57, a. 4, §1.

Secrets can be known by their effects.
I, q. 57, a. 4.

To reveal secrets to the evil of an individual is against fidelity, but not if they are revealed for the sake of the public good, which is always to be preferred to private good.
II-II, q. 68, a. 1, §3.

SECURITY

Security regards the avoidance of evil.
I-II, q. 50, a. 8, §1.

SEDITION

The unity to which sedition is opposed is a unity of law and public utility. Therefore sedition is a mortal sin of its kind. The sin of sedition attaches primarily to those who bring out the sedition; secondarily, to those who abet them in disturbing the common weal.

II-II, q. 42, a. 2.

SEED

The seed, though generating an animal, stems from a previous animal.

I, q. 4, a. 1, §2.

SEEMLINESS

On grounds of moral seemliness one man owes to another a declaration of the truth.

II-II, q. 109, a. 3.

SELF-ABASEMENT

It is quite possible for man unduly to abase himself on some points, and lift himself aloft on others.

II-II, q. 133, a. 1, §3.

SELF-CONFIDENCE

By the self-confidence here set down to be a part of fortitude, a man has hope in himself, yet under God.

II-II, q. 128, a. 1, §2.

One should have a prompt and ready mind for the attack; and to this Tully assigns self-confidence.

II-II, q. 128, a. 1,

Though self-confidence and magnificence are assigned to the doing or attacking of great businesses other than those that are the proper matter of fortitude, still they have a certain affinity on the score of danger imminent.

II-II, q. 128, a. 1, §3.

SELF-CONSCIOUSNESS

A man can understand that he understands.

I, q. 28, a. 4, §2.

Man is conscious that he himself understands.

I, q. 76, a. 1.

SELF-DEFENSE

If any one uses greater violence than is necessary for the defense

172

of his life, it will be unlawful. But if he repels the violence in a moderate way, it will be a lawful defense.
II-II, q. 64, a. 7.

In him who defends himself the act may be without sin, if he defends himself with the mere purpose of repelling the wrong offered, and with due moderation.
II-II, q. 41, a. 1.

SELF-DEPRECIATION

It may happen that men attribute to themselves lower endowments than are really theirs.
II-II, q. 113, a. 1.

One way of attributing to oneself less endowments than one has, contains a departure from truth, as when a person avers of himself some meanness, which he does not recognize in himself, or denies of himself some greatness, which at the same time he perceives to be in himself: this is a piece of self-depreciation which is always sinful.
II-II, q. 113, a. 1.

SELF-ESTEEM

Sometimes a man speaks of himself, not above what he is in himself, but above what men think of him.
II-II, q. 112, a. 1.

Usually it is in consequence of a person being inwardly lifted up by arrogant esteem of himself above his merits, that he outwardly boasts of himself to excess.
II-II, q. 112, a. 1, §2.

SELF-EVIDENCE

Those truths are self-evident which are recognized at once, as soon as the terms in which they are expressed are known.
C.G. I, 10, §1.

SELF-HATE

Properly speaking, it is impossible for any one to hate himself. For naturally everything seeks good, and cannot seek for itself anything except in the light of good.
I-II, q. 29, a. 4.

SELF-KNOWLEDGE

It is a point of the perfection of man that he should know himself.
II-II, q. 132, a. 1, §3.

It is no sin to recognize and approve of your own good qualities.
II-II, q. 132, a. 1.

SELF-LOVE

Naturally everything loves itself, and consequently everything naturally preserves itself in being, and resists destroying agencies as much as it can.
II-II, q. 64, a. 5.

There is well-ordered self-love, due and natural, whereby a man wishes for himself the good that befits him; but the love that is set down as a cause of sin is an inordinate self-love.
I-II, q. 77, a. 4, §1.

It is natural to every one to love his own life, and aids to life, in due measure, which means that these things be not so loved as that a man should set up his rest in them finally, but they should be loved as things that have to be used for the ultimate goal.
II-II, q. 126, a. 1.

SELF-PRESERVATION

It is natural to everything to preserve itself in being as much as it can.
II-II, q. 64, a. 7.

Men are wont to make light of kinsmen and possessions, and even to suffer bodily agonies, to save their lives.
II-II, q. 124, a. 4.

SELF-SUBSISTENCE

Subsisting existence is not created existence.
I, q. 7, a. 2, §1.

SELF-SUFFICIENCY

One of the conditions of happiness is that it should be self-sufficient: otherwise it could not do the office of a supreme goal in setting desire to rest.
II-II, q. 118, a. 7.

Single man is not self-sufficient for the purposes of life.
II-II, q. 129, a. 6.

SELF-UNDERSTANDING

The understanding is perfected in its own understanding.
I, q. 87, a. 3.

SELLING

No one ought to sell to another that which is not his, though he may sell the loss that he suffers.
II-II, q. 77, a. 1.

To sell a thing dearer or buy it cheaper than it is worth, is a proceeding in itself unjust.
II-II, q. 77, a. 1.

SEMEN
The natural generation of man is from semen.
I, q. 92, a. 4.

SENATE
It is said that in the case of a man losing his seat in the senate it is his dignity rather than his status that is taken away from him.
II-II, q. 183, a. 1.

SENSATION
Sensation constitutes a vital function.
I, q. 51, a. 3, §2.

Sensation is the affection of sense.
I, q. 17, a. 2, §1.

One can be deceived about the sensed thing, but not about the fact of sensation.
I, q. 17, a. 2, §1.

Sensation and impression often cause change in the human body.
I, q. 75, a. 3.

SENSE
The senses know the sweet, the white, and so forth.
I, q. 59, a. 1.

The sense delights in objects properly proportioned.
I, q. 5, a. 4, §1.

Sense is found in all animals, but animals other than man have no intellect.
C.G. II, 46, §1.

The apprehension of sense does not extend to the intellectual consideration of the proportion of one thing to another.
II-II q. 58, a. 4.

SENSUALITY
Sensuality does not observe reason.
I, q. 81, a. 3.

SENTENCE, JUDICIAL
A judge's sentence should be fraught with coercive power, whereby both parties may be bound to observe the sentence of the judge: otherwise the judgment would not be effectual.
II-II, q. 67, a. 1.

The tenor of no man's sentence is that he should put himself to death, but that he should suffer death.
II-II, q. 69, a. 4, §2.

SET OF VALUES
Of things to be shunned, some are more to be shunned than others; and of things to be sought, some are more to be sought than others.
II-II, q. 125, a. 1.

SETTLEMENT
A just settlement is some work made adequate to another work according to some measure of equality.
II-II, q. 57, a. 2.

SEX
It is in the union of the bodies that sexual pleasure consists.
II-II, q. 151, a. 2.

Sex is common to animal and man.
I, q. 92, a. 2.

The body is characterized by a male or female sex, whereas the soul is made in the spiritual image of God.
I, q. 91, a. 4.

SHAME
Shame is reckoned to be the opposite of honor and glory.
II-II, q. 142, a. 4.

Shame has regard to the unsightliness of sin: hence a man is not always more ashamed of the more grievous sin, but of that which looks uglier. Hence a man is more ashamed of flattery than of the spirit of contradiction, though the spirit of contradiction is the more grievous.
II-II, q. 116, a. 2, §3.

SHELLFISH
A shellfish moves by expanding and contracting.
I, q. 18, a. 3.

A shellfish has only the sense of touch.
I, q. 18, a. 3.

SHORTCOMING
The knowledge of one's own shortcoming belongs to humility.
II-II, q. 161, a. 2.

SHRILLNESS
Shrillness and rapidity of utterance belong to those who are ready to contend on any question that occurs, which is not the habit of magnanimous men: they meddle only with big things.
II-II, q. 129, a. 3, §3.

SICKNESS

Being insensible to anything sweet, the sick tongue tastes everything as bitter.
I, q. 75, a. 2.

SIGHT

The sight is the most excellent and the most spiritual sense.
I, q. 78, a. 3.

Other things being equal, sight is more certain than hearing.
II-II, q. 4, a. 8, §2.

SIGHT, INTELLECTUAL

The word *sight* is also applied to the invisible knowledge obtained through the intellect or the intellectual eye. And thus it is with the expression *light*.
I, q. 67, a. 1.

SIMPLE

We know simple things by means of composite things.
I, q. 10, a. 1.

SIMPLICITY

Not seeking things too dainty and far-fetched: thereunto simplicity is assigned.
II-II, q. 143, a. 1.

SIMULATION

Simulation is properly a lie enacted in certain signs, consisting of outward actions.
II-II, q. 111, a. 1.

SIN

Freedom from sin is true freedom.
II-II, q. 183, a. 4.

The slavery of sin is repugnant to spiritual liberty.
II-II, q. 147, a. 3, §3.

Real bondage is the bondage of sin.
II-II, q. 183, a. 4.

Sins of the spirit are more culpable than sins of the flesh.
I-II, q. 73, a. 5.

Sin occurs in the reason.
I-II, q. 74, a. 6.

The consummation of sin is in the consent of reason.
II-II, q. 35, a. 3.

By theologians sin is considered principally as an offense against

divine reason; but by the moral philosopher, as an act contrary to human reason.
I-II, q. 71 a. 6, §5.

The assault of sin is sometimes to be overcome by flight, sometimes by resistance; by flight, when continued thinking of the matter increases the incentive to sin; by resistance, when keeping on the thought takes away the incentive to sin.
II-II, q. 35, a. 1, §4.

Sin is a vicious act.
I-II, q. 59, a. 1, §2.

Sins of word are to be judged principally by the intention of the speaker.
II-II, q. 73, a. 2.

Sins of speech have some palliation, since they arise easily by a slip of the tongue without malice prepense.
II-II, q. 73, a. 3.

Sins openly committed come sometimes of greater contempt.
II-II, q. 116, a. 2, §2.

One sin may be the cause of another, as one human act may be the cause of another.
I-II, q. 75, a. 4.

A man ought not to commit one sin to avoid another; and therefore he ought not in any way to lie to avoid pride.
II-II, q. 113, a. 1, §3.

A man ought not to sin against another, simply because that other has first sinned against him.
II-II, q. 108, a. 1.

The sins that do personal hurt are more grievous than sins against property.
II-II, q. 73, a. 3.

When a soul is disordered by sin to the extent of turning away from its last end, that is, from God, then is the sin mortal; but when the disorder stops short of turning away from God, the sin is venial.
I-II, q. 72, a. 5.

When a whole people sins, vengeance is to be taken upon them either to the extent of the whole people, or to the extent of a great portion of the people.
II-II, q. 108, a. 1, §5.

Sins are not imputed to people out of their mind.
II-II, q. 142, a. 3.

A sleeper's violation of the moral law is not imputed to him as sin.
I, q. 84, a. 8.

If the world were deprived of all sin, it would be imperfect. For the common good would disappear, if the individual sin were destroyed, which occasions individual good.
I, q. 82, a. 2, §3. Vide Theodicy.

SINGER

If a good singer loves a good writer, there comes out there a likeness of proportion, inasmuch as each has the gift that benefits him in his own profession.
I-II, q. 27, a. 3, §2.

SINNER

We ought in sinners to hate their being sinners, and love their being men, capable of happiness.
II-II, q. 25, a. 6.

They who sin turn away from that in which the character of the goal is truly found, but not from the simple intention of the final goal, which they mistakenly seek in the wrong things.
I-II, q. 1, a. 7, §1.

The slaying of the sinner becomes lawful in reference to the good of the community that is destroyed by sin.
II-II, q. 64, a. 6.

The sinner by sinning can do no effective hurt to God.
I-II, q. 47, a. 1, §1.

SLAVE

The slave, as a slave, is his master's chattel. But considered as a man, he is something subsisting by himself.
II-II, q. 57, a. 4, §2.

A man is not made free by the mere fact of ceasing to serve, as we see in the case of runaway slaves: but he is properly a slave who is bound to serve; and he is free, who is released from servitude.
II-II, q. 184, a. 4.

SLAVERY

The slavery by which man is subject to man reaches to the body, not to the soul, which remains free.
II-II, q. 104, a. 6, §1.

Slavery is an obstacle to the good use of power, and therefore men naturally shun it.
I-II, q. 2, a. 4, §3.

SLAYING

When from the slaying of the wicked there arises no danger to the good, but rather protection and deliverance, then the wicked may be lawfully slain.
II-II, q. 64, a. 2, §1.

SLEEP

There is no moral evil in sleep taken according to reason.
I-II, q. 34, a. 1, §1.

The senses of the sleeper are suspended because of his exhalations and evaporations.
I, q. 84, a. 8, §2.

The judgment of the sleeper's intellect is sometimes unfettered, according to his sense and imagination being free.
I, q. 84, a. 8, §2. Vide waking up.

The sleeper sometimes distinguishes between dream and reality.
I, q. 84, a. 8, §2.

In the sleeping state the reason has not the free judgment. For there is no sleeper who does not take fantastic images of realities for the realities themselves. And therefore what a man does asleep, is not imputed to him to blame, as neither in that which a madman does.
II-II, q. 154, a. 5.

A man who falls asleep after indulging in food has no phantasms.
I, q. 84, a. 8, §2.

SLIGHT

To an angry man it is pleasant to punish, in that he thinks himself to be removing an apparent slight, coming of a previous offence; for when one is offended by another, he thinks himself slighted thereby, and therefore he desires to be rid of this slight by paying back the offence that he has sustained.
I-II, q. 32, a. 6, §3.

SLOTH

Sloth is a heaviness and sadness, that so weighs down the soul that it has no mind to do anything. It carries with it a disgust of work. It is a torpor of the mind neglecting to set about good. Such sadness is always evil.
II-II, q. 35, a. 1.

SMITH

A smith gathers general knowledge about the knife in order to produce individual knives.
I, q. 84, a. 8.

SOBRIETY

A sober man does not like less food than a glutton, but he curbs his appetite.
I, q. 98, a. 2, §3.

Sobriety is especially required in young men and in women.
II-II, q. 149, a. 6.

SOCIAL

Man is a social being.
I-II, q. 96, a. 4, §1.

A social order cannot be maintained without the authority of one who attends to the common good; for many strive for many things, while one takes care only of one.
I, q. 96, a. 4.

A peaceful state of society is better ensured under private ownership, every one being contented with his own lot.
II-II, q. 66, a. 2.

The order of justice requires that inferiors obey their superiors; otherwise the state and condition of human society could not be preserved.
II-II, q. 104, a. 6.

In consequence of the unity of human society one man ought to be solicitous for another that he sin not.
II-II, p. 108, a. 4, §1.

It is sufficient provision for human society, if some lay their strength in carnal generation, while others, abstaining from that, apply themselves to the contemplation of divine (spiritual) things.
II-II, q. 152, a. 2, §1.

There must be in human society some men devoted to temporal affairs.
C.G. I, 4, §1.

Because man is a social animal, one man naturally owes another that without which human society could not go on.
II-II, p. 3, §1.

Human society could not be maintained without the prohibition of murder, theft, and the like.
I-II, q. 96, a. 2.

SOLDIER

The vocation of a soldier is not only to wear armor, but also to fight.
I, q. 24, a. 2.

Soldiers, by practice of arms and exercise, do not think much of the dangers of war, reckoning their skill sufficient for their security.
II-II, q. 123, a. 1, §2.

SOLEMNITY

Some solemnity is gone through in transactions that are meant to stand and endure perpetually amongst men.
II-II, q. 184, a. 4.

SOLICITUDE

Solicitude implies an earnestness of effort applied to the gaining of a purpose. Clearly a greater earnestness of effort is applied where there is fear of a failure: and where there is secure confidence of success, less solicitude comes in.
II-II, q. 55, a. 6.

Every time has its befitting solicitude, as summer brings the solicitude of reaping, and autumn the solicitude of gathering in the fruit. Any one who in summer-time was already solicitous about gathering in the fruit, would be idly anticipating the solicitude of time to come.
II-II, q. 55, a. 7.

Solicitude for temporal things may be unlawful.
II-II, q. 55, a. 6.

SON

A mature son equals his father.
I, q. 25, a. 6, §2.

SORROW

Sorrow is good in point of its being a recognition of and shrinking from evil.
I-II, q. 39, a. 2.

That pain alone which is caused by an interior apprehension is called sorrow.
I-II, q. 35, a. 2.

SOUL

The soul has a proper function, consisting in the understanding.
I, q. 89, a. 1.

The operation of the sensitive soul, and not of the spiritual soul, belongs to a corporeal organ.
I, q. 75, a. 3. Vide Understanding.

The soul operates through corporeal organs.
I, q. 54, a. 5.

The human soul is always united to the human body.
I, q. 51, a. 1.

The human soul is not corporeal, although united to the body.
I, q. 76, a. 1, §4.

An animal has a sensitive soul, a man an intellectual soul.
I, q. 76, a. 3.

While the animal soul knows only bodies, the human soul can understand divine or spiritual values.
I, q. 75, a. 6, §1.

There is no virtue in the body, but only in the soul.
I-II, q. 56, a. 4, §3.

SOUL AND BODY

Both soul and body are parts of the human nature.
I, q. 91, a. 4, §3.

SOUND

Sound is caused by the motion and percussion of the air.
I, q. 78, a. 3.

SOVEREIGN

The sovereign is not released from the law as regards its directive force, but ought voluntarily, and not of constraint, to fulfil the law.
I-II, q. 96, a. 5, §3.

SPECIES

More or less does not make a difference of species.
I-II, q. 18, a. 11, §4.

SPECTACLE

He who coming first to a public spectacle should prepare the way for the others, would not act unlawfully; but it is then that a person acts unlawfully, when he prevents others from seeing.
II-II, q. 66, a. 2, §2.

SPECULATION

In speculation the perfection and correctness of the procedure depends on the principles whence reason argues.
I-II, q. 57, a. 4.

In matters of speculation the most grievous and most shameful error is in things of which man has knowledge furnished him by nature.
II-II q. 154, a. 12.

SPEECH

Speech is an expression of the intellect.
I, q. 58, a. 4.

Speech is a function of a living being.
I, q. 51, a. 3.

In the usage of human speech some common nouns are restricted to that which is principal in the class denoted by them: as the name of *the City* is understood eminently of Rome.
II-II, q. 141, a. 2.

Speech holds the foremost place among signs.
II-II, 110, a. 1, §2.

SPIRATION

The procession of the consequence from the reason, which is not a physical generation of an effect from a cause, can be called spiration or spiritual generation.
I, q. 27, a. 4, §3.

Spiration or spiritual generation has remained without a name.
I, 2, 27, a. 4, §3.

SPIRIT

In the natural body the different members are kept together in unity by the virtue of the quickening spirit, on the departure of which the members of the body break up.
II-II, q. 183, a. 2, §3.

The spirit requires a corporeal instrument (without becoming itself corporeal).
I, q. 51, a. 1, §1.

SPIRITUAL

Spiritual matters cannot be affected by corporeal, but only by spiritual influences. For a thing can be affected only by similar things.
I, q. 63, a. 2.

SPIRITUAL VALUE

Plato assumed that spiritual values exist besides material things.
I, q. 76, a. 2, §4.

SPORT

Sport and play are necessary to the business of human life.
II-II, q. 168, a. 3.

Because sport is useful for rest and pleasure, and pleasure and rest are not things to be sought for their own sake in human life, but as aids to work, therefore defect in the disposition to sport and play is less of a vice than excess in the same.
II-II, q. 168, a. 4.

184

Sport and play are forbidden to penitents, because mourning is enjoined upon them for their sins.
II-II, q. 168, a. 4, §1.

SQUANDERING

The prodigal sins against himself, squandering his own goods on which he ought to live: he also sins against his neighbor, squandering the goods out of which he ought to provide for others.
II-II q. 119, a. 3, §1.

STAIN, MATERIAL AND SPIRITUAL

A stain properly so called is spoken of in material things, when some lustrous body loses its lustre by contact with another body, as in the case of clothes, gold and silver, and the like. This is the image that must be kept to when we speak of a stain in spiritual things. Now the soul of man has a lustre from the shining of the light of reason. But when it sins, it clings to objects in despite of the light of reason. It is just this loss of lustre, that is called metaphorically a stain on the soul.
I-II, q. 86, a. 1.

STANDARD, NORMATIVE

The divine principle is a normative standard for all men, and not for God. It is a value idea.
I, q. 15, a. 1, §2.

STAR

The rays of the stars have diverse effects.
I, q. 67, a. 3.

STATE

A state is a perfect community.
II-II, q. 65, a. 2, §2.

The state is said to do what the king does, as though the king were the whole state.
I-II, q. 29, a. 4.

As the individual is part of the household, so the household is part of the state; and the state is a perfect community.
I-II, q. 90, a. 3, §3.

STATUE

A statue resembles a man, but not vice versa.
I, q. 4, a. 3, §4.

STATUS

Status properly concerns liberty or slavery, whether in spiritual or in civil matters.
II-II, q. 183, a. 1.

That alone is considered to belong to a man's status, which regards the obligation of his own person, as he is his own master or in the power of another, and that not for any light or easily changeable cause, but on some permanent ground.
II-II, q. 183, a. 1.

Status properly points to a man's condition as freeman or slave.
II-II, q. 184, a. 4.

STATUTE

General statutes are set forth according as they suit the generality.
II-II, q. 147, a. 4.

STEADINESS

Steadiness properly belongs to the habit of virtue.
I-II, q. 100, a. 9.

STEALTH

If all men promiscuously were to steal, human society would be lost.
II-II, q. 66, a. 6.

Whoever takes by stealth his own property from another, in whose hands it is unjustly detained, sins against general justice, usurping the office of judge in his own cause, in disregard of the due course of law.
II-II, q. 66, a. 5.

STERNNESS

Sternness seems to be the quality of a mind that makes no scruple of putting others to pain.
II-II, q. 157, 8.

STRATAGEM

The goal of stratagems is to deceive the enemy.
II-II, q. 40, a. 3.

STRENGTH

Human strength is limited.
I-II, q. 32, a. §3.

STRIKING

He who strikes another is bound to make compensation for the injury to the sufferer, although nothing remains in his possession.
II-II, q. 62, a. 6.

STUDIOUSNESS

Studiousness is properly said to be about knowledge.
II-II, q. 166, a. 1.

STUDY

Study properly implies a vigorous application of the mind to some object.
II-II, q. 166, a. 1.

STUMBLING BLOCK

An obstacle set in the way, so that one is likely to fall over it, is called stumbling block.
II-II, q. 43, a. 1.

STUPIDITY

Though no one wishes to be stupid, still people do wish for what leads to stupidity, by withdrawing their thoughts from things spiritual and burying them in things of earth.
II-II, q. 46, a. 2, §2.

Stupidity implies a dulness of perception in judging, particularly about the supreme reason, the ultimate goal and the highest good.
II-II, q. 46, a. 2.

Stupidity may come of natural incapacity, and that is not a sin. Or it may come of a man burying his mind so deep in earthly things as to render his perceptions unfit to grasp the things of God.
II-II, q. 46, a. 2.

SUBJECT

To rule and govern is not the office of the subject, inasmuch as he is a subject, but rather to be ruled and governed.
II-II, q. 47, a. 12.

SUCCESSION

Succession happens in all movements.
I, q. 10, a. 1.

SUFFERING

A man should not be wearied out by protracted suffering of difficulties, and brought to the point of desisting from his enterprise.
II-II, q. 128, a. 1.

SUICIDE

Even they who kill themselves do so from love of their flesh, which they wish to deliver from present hardship.
II-II, q. 126, a. 1.

Suicide is a sin in regard to oneself.
II-II, q. 64, a. 5.

Every man is of the community; and so what he is, is of the community: hence in killing himself he does an injury to the community.
II-II, q. 64, a. 5.

Suicide is the greatest crime.
II-II, q. 64, a. 5, §3.

No time is left to expiate suicide by repentance.
II-II, q. 64, a. 5, §3.

To kill oneself is altogether unlawful.
II-II, q. 64, a. 5.

SUMMER

Summer brings the solicitude of reaping.
II-II, q. 55, a. 7.

SUN

The size of the sun exceeds that of the earth.
I, q. 85, a. 6.

The whole horizon is illuminated the moment the sun rises.
I, q. 67, a. 2.

The sun resembles everything generated by her.
I, q. 4, a. 2.

SUPERFLUOUS

There are two ways in which a thing may be called superfluous. In one way in point of absolute quantity; in another way, a thing may be superfluous in point of quantity of proportion, because it is not proportionate to the end.
II-II, q. 93, a. 2.

SUPERIOR

They who bear authority count as superiors in respect of those over whom they have received authority, whether ordinary or delegated.
II-II, q. 67, a. 1.

SUPERSTITION

Superstition is a vice opposed to religion in point of excess, not that it renders more to divine worship than true religion does, but because it pays divine worship either to the wrong object, or in some way in which it ought not to be paid.
II-II, q. 92, a. 1.

It will be superstitious and unlawful, if letters are brought in, or names, or any other vain observances, which manifestly have no natural efficiency in the case.
II-II, q. 96, a. 2, §1.

SUPREME COURT
In every judgment the final sentence belongs to the supreme court.
I-II, q. 74, a. 7.

SURFACE
Surface is an attribute of any finite body.
I, q. 7, a. 3.

SURGEON
The surgeon amputates a member of the body in order to save the body.
I, q. 48, a. 6.

The amputation of an unsound limb belongs to the surgeon.
II-II, q. 64, a. 3.

SURMISE
Some acts of the intellect involve thinking without firm assent, inclining rather to one side, but on slight indication, as in surmise.
II-II, q. a. 1.

SURVIVAL, INTELLECTUAL
The intellectual work survives its creator retaining its own existence.
I, q. 76, a. 2, §2.

SUSPICION
Suspicion is an evil opinion entertained on slight grounds.
II-II, q. 60, a. 3.

Suspicion involves a moral flaw in him who harbors it; and the further the suspicion goes, the greater the vice.
II-II, q. 60, a. 3.

When you despise or hate a person, or are angry with him or envy him, you are apt to think evil of him upon slight indications.
II-II, q. 60, a. 3.

SUSTENANCE
Bodily sustenance is taken by actions that give pleasure.
II-II, q. 142, a. 1, §2.

SUUM CUIQUE
The proper act of justice is nothing else than to render suum cuique.
II-II, q. 58, a. 11.

SWALLOW
Every swallow builds its nest in the same way.
C.G. II, 46, §1.

SWEARING
To call God to witness is to swear, sometimes about things present or past, sometimes in confirmation of a future performance.
II-II, q. 89, a. 1.

SWEET
Sweet appears bitter to a sick man.
I, q. 17, a. 2.

SYLLOGISM
The efficient cause of a syllogism is the rational soul forming it, but its matter is the three terms, the remote matter, and two propositions, to proximate matter; its end is to give belief or knowledge of the unknown conclusion, its form is the virtue or power of inferring the conclusion from the premises.
I. q. 54, a. 2, I-II q. 57, a. 3 I-II, q. 102, a. 6.

In syllogisms leading to an impossible conclusion, sometimes the error is brought home to one by his being landed in a more manifest absurdity.
II-II, q. 162, a. 6, §3.

In syllogistic disputation, given one absurdity, others must follow.
I-II, q. 19, a. 6, §3.

SYMPATHY
Sympathy is a simple act of the will by which we wish well to another, not presupposing the union of affection.
II-II, q. 27, a. 2.

SYNDERESIS
Synderesis is the habitual inclination towards the good.
I, q. 79, a. 12.

SYNONYM
Synonyms denote the same concept.
I, q. 13, a. 4.

T

TAKING
Whoever is a cause of wrongful taking, is bound to restitution.
II-II, q. 62, a. 7.

TASTE
Located only in the tongue, taste can without difficulty be distinguished from touch.
I, q. 78, a. 3, §3.

TEACHER
Whatever is put into the disciple's mind by the teacher is contained in the knowledge of the teacher, unless the teacher is teaching dishonestly.
C.G. I, 7, §2.

TEARS
Tears and groans naturally assuage sorrow.
I-II q. 38, a. 2.

TEETH
The whiteness of a man's teeth primarily belongs, not to him, but to them.
I, q. 8, a. 4.

TEMPERANCE
Temperance is a curb of the passions which incite to something against reason.
I-II, q. 61, a. 2.

Temperance is about desires and delights.
II-II, q. 141, a. 4.

Temperance clearly is not contrary to the inclination of human nature, but in accordance with it.
II-II, q. 141, a. 1, §1.

Temperance is a disposition of mind, which sets bounds to all manner of passions or actions, that they may not exceed.
I-II, q. 61, a. 4.

It belongs to temperance to bridle delights that overmuch allure the soul to go after them.
II-II, q. 146, a. 1, §3.

TEMPLE
It is God's privilege to have a temple.
I, q. 27, a. 1.

TEMPTATION
This life cannot be lived without human temptation.
II-II, q. 60, a. 3.

A man tempts God sometimes in words, sometimes in deeds.
II-II, q. 97, a. 1.

TERMINUS
A terminus may be either a final terminus and point of rest, the terminus of the whole movement, or it may be some intermediate stage, the beginning of one portion of the movement, and the end or terminus of another.
I-II, q. 12, a. 2.

TERRIBLE
That alone is terrible which has an exterior cause.
I-II, q. 52, a. 3.

THEFT
The proper essence of theft is a secret taking of another's property.
II-II, q. 66, a. 3.

To use the property of another, taking it secretly, in a case of extreme need, cannot properly speaking be characterized as theft.
II-II, q. 66, a. 7, §2.

THEODICY
The order of the moral world requires that there should be some failing beings. Vide Sin.
I, q. 49, a. 2.

The divine providence permits defects in certain things, in order not to hinder the perfect things: if all evil were prevented, also the good would be absent. The lion could not live, if he

could not kill other animals; and there would not be patient martyrs without persecuting tyrants.
I, q. 22, a. 2, §2.

Many good things would disappear if God would abolish evil. The retributive justice and the patience of a sufferer could not be praised if there were not injustice.
I, q. 48, a. 2, §3.

In intending justice God also wills punishment besides reward, as in wishing the preservation of the natural order He also wills some natural things corrupted.
I, q. 19, a. 9.

The sinner does not intend any justice (which as just punishment still accompanies his sin).
I, q. 19, a. 9, §1.

God provides for all things (good and bad).
I, q. 22, a. 2, §2.

Evil is known from the good, and vice versa.
I, q. 48, a. 1.

The perfection of the moral world requires corruptible besides incorruptible beings, malefactors besides benefactors.
I, q. 48, a. 2.

Defect and decay in natural things are contrary to perfection and growth of them, yet they are in harmony with the plan of the natural universe, inasmuch as the defect in one thing causes the perfection of another. The species continues, if the decline of one thing gives place to the generation of another.
I, q. 22, a. 2, §2.

The tyrant does not intend that the patience of the martyrs should shine forth (which still follows their persecutions).
I, q. 19, a. 9, §1.

Although evil is not good and not intended by God, it must happen, because it achieves some good end.
I, q. 19, a. 9, §1.

To preserve the wheat, that is, the good, our Lord has commanded us to abstain from rooting out the cockle, teaching us rather to let the wicked live than to let the good be slain with them.
II-II, q. 64, a. 2, §1.

THEOLOGY

The science to which it belongs to prove the existence of God and other truths concerning Him, is the last of all sciences pro-

posed to man to study, many other sciences being preliminary to it; and thus it were only when much of life was already past that man would arrive at the knowledge of God.
II-II, q. 2, a. 4.

THING

The difference of spiritual and corporeal things has been ascribed by Anaxagoras to the different conditions of reasons and causes.
I, q. 47, a. 1.

All things that can be set right by reason, are the subject-matter of moral virtue.
II-II, q. 58, a. 8.

THING, DIVINE

Men rejoice in tribulations from the contemplation of divine things, and, what is more, even in the midst of bodily tortures such joy is found.
I-II, q. 38, a. 4.

THING, EXTERIOR

An exterior thing may be considered in two ways; in one way in respect of its nature, in another way as regards the use of the thing; and in this way man has natural dominion over exterior things.
II-II, q. 66, a. 1.

THING, INTELLECTUAL

Intellectual things or spiritual values cannot contain matter.
I, q. 50, a. 2.

THING, SENSIBLE

We are ignorant of many properties of the things of sense; and of the properties that our senses do apprehend, in most cases we cannot perfectly discover the cause.
C.G. I, 3, §1.

The proper subject-matter of the intellect is the sensible thing.
I, q. 84, a. 8.

THING, SPIRITUAL

A spiritual thing cannot have its equivalent in any earthly price.
II-II, q. 100, a. 1.

THINKING

By right thinking in the more proper sense of the word we mean an intellectual study, attended with inquiry, prior to arriving at a perfect understanding by certitude of vision; or, a movement

of the mind deliberating, and not yet made perfect by a full vision of the truth.
II-II, q. 2, a. 1.

THIRST
One takes pleasure in drinking because he is troubled with thirst, but when the thirst is wholly driven away, the pleasure of drinking likewise ceases.
I-II, q. 35, a. 5.

THOUGHT
Thoughts are expressed by countenance as well as by acts.
I, q. 57, a. 4.

THROWING
What a man wants to throw far, he raises aloft.
II-II, q. 112, a. 1.

TIME
Time is the measure of the movement of natural phenomena.
I, q. 85, a. 4, §1.

Some say that time has no beginning.
I, q. 46, a. 3.

No work can be virtuous unless it be clothed in due circumstances, one of which is due time.
II-II, q. 55, a. 7.

Everything must necessarily be weakened by time, the cause of which is impaired by time.
I-II, q. 48, a. 2, §2.

The things that are in time are measured in a manner by the duration of time.
I-II, q. 52, a. 6.

TIMIDITY
Timidity is opposed to fortitude by excess of fear.
II-II, q. 126, a. 2.

TOUCH
The better the intellect, the better the sense of touch.
I, q. 76, a. 5.

TRACE
The imprints of animal feet are called traces.
I, q. 93, a. 6.

TRADE
Trade too much entangles the soul in secular cares, and withdraws from spirituality.
II-II, q. 77, a. 4, §3.

TRADER

It belongs to traders to be occupied with the exchange of commodities.
II-II, q. 77, a. 4.

TRANSCENDENTALISM

God being spiritual transcends the whole material world, but comprises the whole moral world.
I, q. 61, a. 3, §2.

TRANSGRESSION

Transgression properly means acting against a negative precept. It is distinguished from omission, which is against an affirmative precept.
II-II, q. 79, a. 2.

TREACHERY

Sins that are committed by treachery look worse, because they appear to have their origin in weakness and a certain falseness of reason.
II-II, q. 116, a. 2, §2.

TRIANGLE

No pleasure gets in the way of our understanding the truth that the three angles of a triangle are altogether equal to two right angles.
I-II, q. 33, a. 3.

TRUTH

The object of the intellect is universal truth.
I-II, q. 2, a. 8.

Truth is the conformity of intellect and thing.
I, q. 16, a. 2.

The truth is the same, be it understood by one or many intellects.
I, q. 76, a. 2, §4.

The truth refers to knowledge.
I, q. 16, a. 3.

Truth and falsehood do not exist in things, except in relation to intellect.
I, q. 17, a. 1.

The discovery of truth is the fruit of studious enquiry.
C.G. I, 4, §1.

Truth offers itself to consideration in two shapes: in the shape of something known of itself, and in the shape of something

known through something else. What is known of itself is a principle perceived by the intellect at a glance. The truth that is known through something else is gathered by inquiry of reason, and stands as the termination of a reasoning process.
I-II, q. 57, a. 2.

Truth is defined by the equation of thought and thing.
I, q. 16, a. 1.

A man owes by a certain moral fitness that declaration of truth to other men with which human society could not endure.
II-II, q. 114, a. 2, §1.

He who speaks the truth, utters certain signs conformable to things, the signs being either words or outward deeds or any outward things whatever.
II-II, q. 109, a. 1, §3.

TRUTH AND GOOD
Truth and good imply one another: the truth is good, and the good is true. *Vide* Goodness, Introduction.
I, q. 79, a. 11, §2.

TRUTHFULNESS
Truthfulness is a moral virtue.
II-II, q. 109, a. 1, §3.

It belongs to the virtue of truthfulness that one should show himself exteriorly by outward signs to be such as he really is.
II-II, q. 110, a. 1.

There is a certain special order whereby our outward behavior whether in word or deed is ordained as a sign to something signified; and to this effect man is perfected by the virtue of truthfulness.
II-II, q. 109, a. 2.

U

UNBELIEF
Judgment on matters of faith is corrupted by unbelief.
II-II, q. 162, a. 4.

The sin of unbelief is greater than all sins of moral perversity.
II-II, q. 10, a. 3.

Unbelief is a mortal sin.
I-II, q. 74, a. 10.

UNDERSTANDING
Understanding is an entirely immaterial or spiritual cognition.
I, q. 50, a. 2.

Aristotle maintained that understanding is performed without the help of a corporeal organ.
I, q. 75, a. 3.

Understanding and reason are incorporeal.
I, q. 3, a. 1, §2.

The act of understanding does not appear externally, but remains internal.
I, q. 14, a. 4.

To understand is an act of an intelligent being, existing in that being, not passing out to anything external.
C.G. I, 45, §1.

The practical understanding has a good which is outside of itself, but the speculative understanding has a good within itself, to wit, the contemplation of truth.
I-II, q. 3, a. 5, §2.

The apprehension of sense does not extend to the consideration of the proportion of one thing to another: that is proper to understanding.
II-II, q. 58, a. 4.

A man is much more pleased at knowing a thing by understanding it, than at knowing it by feeling it.
I-II, q. 31, a. 5.

To understand something in general, and not in particular, is to have an imperfect understanding.
I, q. 14, a. 6.

For the perfect activity of the understanding there is requisite indeed a withdrawal from this corruptible body, which weighs down the soul, but not from the spiritual body, which will be wholly subject to the spirit.
I-II, q. 4, a. 6, §3.

Human understanding is very much to seek in the things of God, as is shown by the errors and mutual contradictions of philosophers.
II-II, q. 2, a. 4.

An individual can hardly understand all physical phenomena.
I, q. 88, a. 1.

Some persons understand more than others.
I, q. 85, a. 7.

UNDO
Even God cannot make what is done undone.
II-II, q. 152, a. 3, §3.

UNION, SPIRITUAL
The end of spiritual life is the union of man with God: to this end all the other elements of spiritual life are directed as means.
II-II, q. 44, a. 1.

UNITY
The yearning after unity must be set down as a cause of pain. For the good of everything consists in a certain unity, inasmuch as everything has united in itself all the elements of its perfect well-being.
I-II, q. 36, a. 3.

Unity signifies absence of division.
I, q. 92, a. 4.

The order of the spiritual things created by God demonstrates the unity of the religious world.
I, q. 47, a. 3.

Plato proves the unity of the material world from the unity of the exemplary or moral world.
I, q. 47, a. 3, §1.

UNITY, MORAL

The interior act and the exterior are physically different in kind: but out of these different constituents there results a moral unity.
I-II, q. 20, a. 3, §1.

UNIVERSAL

What is abstracted from the concrete things is called universal.
I, q. 86, a. 1.

UNJUST

As it would be unjust to compel a man to observe a law that was not enacted by public authority, so also is it unjust to compel a man to submit to a sentence that is not passed by public authority.
II-II, q. 60, a. 6.

UNNATURAL

It happens occasionally in an individual that some of the principles of the species are corrupted; and thus what is unnatural to the species becomes accidentally natural to this individual.
I-II, q. 31, a. 7.

USEFUL

All articles of possession fall under the category of the useful.
II-II, q. 62, a. 5, §1.

USURY

To take usury for the lending of money is in itself unjust, because it is a case of selling what is non-existent.
II-II, q. 78, a. 1.

V

VAIN
Glory may be called vain, if one does not direct the seeking of it to the due goal, that is, to the neighbor's salvation.
II-II, q. 132, a. 1.

VAINGLORY
Supposing one goes after vainglory, whether he does his duty for vainglory or leaves it undone, he will sin in either case.
I-II, q. 19, a. 6, §3.

VALUE IDEA
It is necessary to assume value ideas in the divine mind.
I, q. 15, a. 1.

By value idea is understood the spiritual value, in contradistinction to the value-free corporeal thing.
I, q. 15, a. 1.

The value idea of God is the divine essence.
I, q. 15, a. 1, §3.

There are many value ideas.
I, q. 15, a. 2.

There exists in the divine mind a value idea to which the religious world should conform.
I, q. 15, a. 1.

One cherishes by faith immaterial value ideas which rest on authority.
I, q. 99, a. 1.

The deepest felicity of man consists, not in the understanding of any (moral or legal) value idea, but in that of the divine value idea.
I, q. 89, a. 2, §3.

We cannot apprehend spiritual value ideas through physical phenomena.
I, q. 88, a. 2.

Man, and not animal, understands value ideas.
I, q. 75, a. 6, §1.

The divine value idea is essentially God.
I, q. 15, a. 1.

A value idea is also called an exemplar.
I, q. 47, a. 5, §2. Vide Idea.

VALUE, SPIRITUAL

We can gain knowledge of spiritual values.
I, q. 10, a. 6.

Spiritual values can be known only through material things.
I, q. 50, a. 3, §3.

The existence of the intellect sufficiently proves that there are spiritual values apprehensible only by the intellect.
I, q. 50, a. 1.

Origen contended that God originally created spiritual values only.
I, q. 65, a. 2.

VANITY

Sometimes it is not arrogance, but a sort of vanity, that moves a man to boasting, and gives him delight therein because that is his way.
II-II, q. 112, a. 1, §2.

VASE

The liquid in a colored glass vase seems to be of the same color.
I, q. 75, a. 2.

VENDOR

If there are secret flaws, and the vendor does not reveal them, he drives an unlawful and treacherous bargain, and is bound to compensate the purchaser for his loss.
II-II, q. 77, a. 3.

VENERATION

The veneration with which we venerate God—a part of divine worship, or latria—is different from the veneration called dulia, with which we honor certain excellent creatures.
II-II, q. 84, a. 1, §1.

VENGEANCE

Vengeance is taken by some penal evil inflicted on the offender.
II-II, q. 108, a. 1.

Vengeance may be sought either well or ill.
II-II, q. 158, a. 1.

If the intention of him who takes vengeance makes principally for some good that is reached by the punishment of the offender, then vengeance may be lawful, other due circumstances being observed.
II-II, q. 108, a. 1.

Vengeance is so far lawful and virtuous, as it makes for the restraint of evil.
II-II, q. 108, a. 3.

The taking of vengeance belongs to justice, and the injuring of any one belongs to injustice.
I-II, q. 46, a. 7.

VICE

The opposite of virtue is vice. Vice is against the nature of man inasmuch as it is against the order of reason.
I-II, q. 71, a. 1, 2.

The general prevalence of sin diminishes the turpitude and infamy of certain vices in the opinion of men, but not in the nature of the vices themselves.
II-II, q. 142, a. 4, §2.

Those vices that have a connatural bearing on the end of any capital vice, are said to be its daughters.
II-II, q. 132, a. 5.

Not all the vices from which the virtuous abstain are prohibited by human law, but only those graver excesses from which it is possible for the majority of the multitude to abstain.
I-II, q. 56, a. 2.

VICE, CAPITAL

That is called a capital vice, from which many vices take their origin.
II-II, q. 158, a. 6.

VIOLENCE

A man may be dragged by violence, but his being so dragged of his own will is inconsistent with the idea of violence.
I-II, q. 6, a. 4.

Violence is against the will of the violated.
I, q. 82, a. 1.

VIRGINITY

Virginity abstains from all sexual pleasures.
I-II, q. 64, a. 1, §s.

It cannot be that he who once has experienced sexual pleasure should come to the condition of never having experienced it.
II-II, q. 152, a. 3, §3.

VIRTUALLY

He who has money has not yet got gain actually, but only virtually.
II-II, q. 62, a. 4, §1.

VIRTUE

God's will is the reason of the virtue of men.
I, q. 20, a. 4, §5.

Acts of virtue ought not to be done anyhow, but with observance of due circumstances requisite to the act being virtuous, so that it be done where it ought, and when it ought, and as it ought.
II-II q. 33, a. 2.

There is a certain beauty of its kind proper to every virtue.
II-II, q. 129, a. 4.

The moral virtues preserve the good of reason against the assaults of passion.
II-II, q. 136, a. 1.

Virtue is a good of the mind.
II-II, q. 26, a. 4, §2.

Virtue is applicable to good alone.
I-II, q. 59, a. 1.

It is of the essence of human virtue to secure in human life attention to rational good, which is the proper good of man.
II-II, q. 129, a. 3.

It belongs to human virtue to make a man good, and his work according to reason.
II-II, q. 123, a. 1.

Virtue denotes some perfection of a power.
I-II, q. 55, a. 1.

The outward act of a virtue is sometimes performed by persons who have not the virtue, or some other motive than the motive of the virtue.
II-II, q. 123, a. 1, §2.

Fitness for virtue is in us by nature, but the fulness of virtue comes by practice.
II-II, q. 108, a. 2.

Virtue is said to be self-sufficient, because it can exist even with-

out exterior goods: nevertheless it needs exterior goods to have more of a free hand in its working.
II-II, q. 129, a. 8, §1.

VIRTUE, MORAL
Moral virtue is the rectification of appetite.
I-II, q. 57, a. 4.

A habit of moral virtue makes a man prompt to choose the golden mean in actions and passions.
I-II, q. 53, a. 3.

VIRTUE, RELIGIOUS
A virtue is said to be religious from having God for the object to which it clings.
II-II, q. 17, a. 6.

The object of the religious virtues is God Himself, the highest value idea of all spiritual values.
I-II, q. 62, a. 2.

Religious virtues, having the ultimate goal for their object, stand above all others.
II-II, q. 169, a. 5.

The measure and rule of the religious virtue is God.
I-II, q. 64, a. 4.

VIRTUOUS
Sometimes, for good to come of it, or for the avoidance of evil, the virtuous man will not shrink from making those sorrowful with whom he associates.
II-II, q. 114, a. 1, §3.

VISION
Vision, the activity of the understanding, is better than delight.
I-II, q. 4, a. 2.

VITAL
Vital operations are those which the operator produces of itself.
I, q. 18, a. 3, §2.

Animals move with vital movements.
I, q. 18, a. 1, §2.

VOLUNTARINESS
Voluntariness in its perfection is within the competence of the rational nature alone, but in an imperfect way it is within the competence even of dumb animals.
I-II, q. 6, a. 2.

There must be a voluntary element in human acts. In evidence of this position, we must consider that, in order to anything being done for an end, there is requisite some sort of knowledge of the end.
I-II, q. 6, a. 1.

VOW

There are three necessary requisites to a vow: deliberation, purpose of the will, and promise; and in this the essence of the vow is complete.
II-II, q. 88, a. 1.

A vow in its own nature is more binding than an oath.
II-II, q. 89, a. 8.

To take a vow is voluntary, but to pay the vow is of necessity.
II-II, q. 10, a. 8, §3.

That which is absolutely necessary to be or not to be, in no way falls under vow. Thus it would be a folly to vow to die, or not to fly into the air.
II-II, q. 88, a. 2.

WAKING UP
Waking up, one realizes the flaws of reasoning while asleep.
I, q. 84, a. 8, §2.

WANTS
It is beyond the condition of man to have no wants at all.
II-II, q. 129, a. 6.

WAR
There are two sorts of just war, one general, as when people fight on a battlefield; the other particular, as when a judge, or even a private person, goes not back upon a just decision for any fear of the sword threatening him, or of any danger even unto death.
II-II, q. 123, a. 5.

It does not belong to a private person to start a war, for he can prosecute his claim in the court.
II-II, q. 40, a. 1.

It is lawful to use stratagems in just wars.
II-II, q. 40, a. 3.

The desperate in war are dangerous on account of a certain hope attaching to their despair. For they who despair of flight are weakened in their efforts to fly, but hope to avenge their death; and therefore in this hope they fight the harder. Hence they prove dangerous to the enemy.
I-II, q. 50, a. 8, §3.

For the defense of the commonwealth, just wars may lawfully be prosecuted on feast-days, if necessity so requires.
II-II, q. 40, a. 4.

When necessity ceases, war is not lawful on feast-days.
II-II, q. 40, a. 4.

WARMING

Warming oneself at the fire suits a man in winter, not in summer.
I-II, q. 32, a. 2.

WATER

A water that has a continuous current is metaphorically called living.
I, q. 18, a. 1, §3.

WEAKNESS

Weakness leads to corruption.
I, q. 77, a. 8.

Weaknesses take small things for great.
II-II, q. 132, a. 2, §1.

WEALTH

Wealth gives a basis for expecting self-sufficiency.
I, q. 26, a. 4.

WEANING

When along with the fault the punishment also becomes known, man's will is thereby weaned from sin; because the punishment terrifies him more than the example of the fault allures him.
II-II, q. 108, a. 3, §3.

WEATHER

It is pleasant to sit by the fire in cold weather, and not otherwise.
I, q. 19, a. 7.

WEEPING

Weeping and groaning are activities that suit a man in sorrow or pain, and therefore they are rendered pleasing to such persons.
I-II, q. 38, a. 2.

WELL-BEING

All men desire the fulness of their own well-being, in which full well-being the last end consists.
I-II, q. 1, a. 7.

WHOLE

Let us contemplate about the whole of the human race as we contemplate about the whole universe.
I, q. 23, a. 5, §3.

WICKEDNESS

One fears to dwell in the company of the wicked, lest by them he be led to sin.
I-II, q. 52, a. 3.

Conscious of his own wickedness, one easily thinks ill of others.
II-II, q. 60, a. 3.

WIDOWHOOD
Widowhood is secondary continence.
II-II, q. 155, a. 1.

WILL
The will follows the apprehension of the intellect or reason.
I-II, q. 5, a. 8, §2.

Will is the name of the rational appetite; and therefore in creatures devoid of reason there can be no will.
I-II, q. 6, a. 2, §1.

The will is the origin of all morality.
I, q. 48, a. 1, §2.

That power of the soul whose act is choice, is the will.
II-II, q. 155, a. 3.

A naturally contingent cause must be determined to act by some external being. The divine will, however, determines itself.
I, q. 19, a. 3, §5.

There is in every intellectual being an intellectual will, as there is in every sensible being a sensible will.
I, q. 19, a. 1.

The will of God is not moved by the will of man, but by itself. This free will is what Plato meant when he declared that the first mover moves himself.
I, q. 19, a. 1. §3.

WILL, DIVINE
The divine will should always be fulfilled.
I, q. 19, a. 6.

The divine will is the reason of all religious things.
I, q. 19, a. 4.

The divine will is reasonable.
I, q. 19, a. 5, §1.

There is nothing antecedent or following in the timeless divine will.
I, q. 19, a. 6, §1.

WILL OF GOD
The will of God is the reason of the virtue of men.
I, q. 20, a. 4.

The divine commandments are metaphorically called the will of God.
I, q. 19, a. 11.

WINE

One should not abstain altogether from wine, but only from the immoderate use of it.
II-II, q. 149, a. 3, §1.

One is easily hurt by wine.
II-II, q. 149, a. 3.

Wine taken in immoderate quantities is a marked hindrance to the use of reason.
II-II, q. 149, a. 6.

WISDOM

Wisdom considers the highest goals, and hence is apt to judge and ordain on all points, because a perfect and universal judgment cannot be got except by carrying matters back to their first reasons.
I-II, q. 57, a. 2.

There is a certain wisdom according to God, that has annexed to it folly in the eyes of the world.
II-II, q. 113, a. 1, §1.

WISE

It belongs to the wise man to be good company to those with whom he converses, not in wantonness that virtue shuns, but with propriety.
II-II, q. 114, a. 1, §3.

To be wise is the same as to understand God.
I, q. 14, a. 4.

The name *wise* without qualification is reserved for him alone who deals with the last goal which is also the first commandment.
C.G. I, 1, §1.

WITNESS

Small indeed seems to be his reverence for God, who brings God in as witness to a light matter, which he would not presume to do with any man of honorable position.
II-II, q. 89, a. 2.

In the dignity of his person, a neighbor is injured secretly by false witness or detraction.
II-II, q. 61, a. 3.

If a judge knows that a party is innocent, whose guilt is being evidenced by false witnesses, he ought to examine the witnesses

more diligently, to find occasion of discharging the unoffending party.
II-II, q. 64, a. 6, §3.

WOMAN
Woman possesses intellect as well as man.
I, q. 93, a. 4, §1.

Woman should be loved by man, being created from him.
I, q. 92, a. 2.

The woman was created as a helper in the work of generation.
I, q. 92, a. 1.

If a married woman dresses well to please her husband, she may do it without sin. But those women who neither have nor want to have husbands, or who are in a state that binds them not to carry, cannot without sin seek to please the eyes of men to make them fall in love with them, because that is to furnish their neighbor with an incentive to sin.
II-II, q. 169, a. 2.

The looking at a woman sometimes makes for lust.
II-II, q. 167, a. 2.

WOMB, CORPORAL AND SPIRITUAL
Indeed at first the son is not distinct in body from his parents, so long as he is contained in his mother's womb. Afterwards when he leaves the womb, before he has the use of reason, he is contained under his parents' care as in a sort of spiritual womb.
II-II, q. 10, a. 12.

WORD
Words are angels, or messengers of the intellect.
1, q. 34, a. 1.

Words also signify spiritual values apprehended by the intellect.
I, q. 13, a. 1.

Words are naturally signs of thoughts.
II-II, q. 110, a. 3.

We address words to a man to express to him the thought of our heart, which he cannot know otherwise than by our words.
II-II, q. 91, a. 1.

Sins of word are weighed principally according to the disposition in which they are uttered.
II-II, q. 76, a. 3.

WORK
Great works cannot be done without great expenses.
II-II, q. 134, a. 3.

WORLD, MATERIAL
Some say that the material world was not created by the spiritual God.
I, q. 46, a. 2, §1.

WORLD, RELIGIOUS
The whole religious world is ordained towards a divine goal.
I, q. 65, a. 2.

The religious or spiritual world cannot be proved by the senses, but by the understanding (which is sufficient in theology).
I, q. 46, a. 2.

That the religious or spiritual world has a beginning, is not an object of natural but of spiritual science.
I, q. 46, a. 1.

WORM
Worms are generated from an animal.
I, q. 27, a. 2.

WORSHIP
Among the marks of reverence that we pay to excellent creatures (or rather creators) the greatest is worship.
II-II, q. 84, a. 1, §1.

Religious worship is not paid to images considered in themselves as things, but inasmuch as they are images leading on to the intelligible God.
II-II, q. 81, a. 3, §3.

Worship consists principally in inward reverence to God, but secondarily in certain corporal signs of humility: thus we bend the knee to mark our weakness in comparison with God; and we fall on our faces to profess that of ourselves we are nothing.
II-II, q. 84, a. 2, §2.

WORTHINESS
The worthiness of a person may be determined from two points of view. In one way, he is the more worthy who abounds more in spiritual gifts. Another way is in reference to the common good; for sometimes the less holy and the less learned may be more

available for the common good, by reason of worldly ability or business capacity, or some other advantage.
II-II, q. 63, a. 2.

WRITING
The writing in a book signifies things to be done.
I, q. 24, a. 1.

WRONG
No one does wrong in using a thing for the purpose for which it exists.
II-II, q. 64, a. 1.

Y

YEARNING
Everything yearns after unity as after goodness; and therefore, in the same way that the yearning after good is a cause of pain, so also is the yearning after unity.
I-II, q. 36, a. 3.

YOUNG
For those young people who are prone to acts of virtue by a good natural disposition, or by custom, the paternal discipline suffices, which is by admonition.
I-II, q. 95, a. 1.

YOUTH
Youths, through the heat of their nature, have high spirits, and so the heart in them is dilated; and from the dilation of the heart it is that one tends to things arduous, and therefore youths are courageous and of good hope. In like manner also they who have not suffered defeat, nor experienced obstacles to their efforts, easily count a thing possible to them.
I-II, q. 50, a. 6.

Sobriety is especially required in young men and in young women.
II-II, q. 149, a. 6.

Youth is a cause of hope. For young men have much of the future before them, and little of the past at their back; and therefore they have little of memory, and live a great deal in hope.
I-II, q. 50, a. 6.

Z

ZEAL

Zeal, whichever way we look at it, comes of intensity of love. For clearly, the greater the intensity wherewith any power tends to an end, the more vigorously does it bear down all opposition or resistance.

I-II, q. 28, a. 4.

RENEWALS 458-4574
DATE DUE

DEC − 6			
NOV 0 8			
NOV 0 9			
NOV 2 5			
GAYLORD			PRINTED IN U.S.A.